Links to podcasts, social media,
and additional content can be found at:

AuthorMannyGarcia.com

Also by Manny Garcia:

***Glossary of Life - A Path to Joy,
Balance, and Peace***

NOT
GOOD ENOUGH
TO BE TRUE

How to Be Happy
in a World Full of Lies

MANNY GARCIA

ISBN: 979-8-9910494-6-7 (Hardcover)
ISBN: 979-8-9910494-7-4 (Paperback)
ISBN: 979-8-9910494-8-1 (eBook)
ISBN: 979-8-9910494-9-8 (Audiobook)

Illustrations by Edson Campos
Audiobook music by Jan Michael Looking Wolf
Cover images purchased through iStock by Getty Images

The most deceptive lies thrive in the theater of our thoughts...

But the highest truths live in the expanse of our feelings.

.

You have been deceived.

But it's okay, we all have... by ourselves and by those around us. We're all doing our best to tell truth from fiction, and our elders and leaders have done their best to teach us what they perceive as truth. But truth isn't pliable and can't be stretched and shaped at our whim. And when we miss it while trying to live by something that isn't true, the inevitable result is discomfort and suffering. Untruths can be sneaky and deceptive, especially when they're in-flated by the power of our beliefs. So often - without any real proof - we believe negative things about ourselves and about life. You'll read things in this book that also offer no tangible proof, but instead invite you to search your own feelings, pay attention to your own experience, and use both to entertain inspiring possibilities you may not have considered before. To achieve this, you'll be prompted to go deeper than mere intellect... beyond your mind and into your heart's intuition.

Things are not as they appear in this world. Circum-stances of grand opportunity in life are frequently camou-flaged as unfortunate events. Truth, however, is always big-ger than negativity. And when something appears negative, it's a sure sign that what you're looking at isn't the whole story and is not good enough to be true. We're all, in our own ways, trying to find a path to higher joy and greater peace. The good news is that we have help on that path. Some of this help is obvious - in the form of those who walk with us through life. But there's much more help available that operates behind the scenes of our five senses. To fully engage that help, we must be open to concepts that may not initially appear logical. Although, the further we look back at recorded history - through humanity's many stages of awareness - the more subjective the term "logical" becomes. Quite a few concepts (especially in science), which were once considered illogical, are now contemporary common sense.

One recurrent theme you'll notice in this book is the notion that you're not here by accident. None of us are. In a way, life is a spiritual gym, and we're all here to get into better shape. Life is also a personal trainer that will push us to some very uncomfortable places for our own benefit. Yet who and what we are in any moment is enough. And this process of growth we're all going through, no matter how convoluted, is always perfect. Through life's ups and downs, the ongoing intention of our journey is to achieve greater joy and higher awareness. The backdrop of that journey is a Universe that the brightest minds in science tell us is far stranger and more mysterious than we can imagine. This is reason for optimism. For all we think we know, we have so much left to discover - both personally and scientifically. And this great unknown is a wonderland where surprise is on our side.

Through these pages, we'll follow together a trail of breadcrumbs that's meant to ground you in a higher truth and lead you back to yourself... to a completeness within that you've perhaps not yet encountered. As you get closer to realizing this completeness, you'll find that it functions as your own private source of wisdom and guidance. You will also discover that a meaningful life boils down to something so much simpler than we've been led to believe.

Wherever you're from and whoever you are, if you're looking to experience greater happiness in life, you must get humble. That's because the doors of discovery are narrow and will not accommodate enlarged egos who aren't open to new perspectives. In that vein of humility, it needs to be said that nothing you read here should be regarded as infallible. This book was written as a tool to help you find *your* truth - not to convince you to accept my truth. That said, my hope is that these ideas will help you through life and that you'll find them thought-provoking, comforting, and encouraging.

Be courageous... be kind... and be well,

- manny

UNTRUTHS

PART ONE: THE LIES WE TELL OURSELVES

PART TWO: THE LIES WE'VE BEEN TOLD

PART ONE:

THE LIES WE TELL OURSELVES

LIE #1: LIFE ISN'T FAIR

The Deception:

Do you remember how old you were when someone first told you that life isn't fair? You were probably very young, and it was likely in response to your frustration over not getting what you wanted. From the time we first believed this lie, many of us have unconsciously used that shortsighted catchphrase to pacify our frustrations or reconcile circumstances we didn't like. The phrase implicates life itself as an unpredictable villain who is at best ignorant of decency and at worst intentionally cruel. It's no wonder many people feel that life is a jungle in which they must fight to survive. Believing that life is inherently unfair amounts to a shallow, catch-all judgment that fails to comprehend a deeper meaning in the way our lives unfold.

The danger that comes with buying into the idea that life isn't fair has a name: resignation. If life isn't fair, why should anyone bother trying to succeed when, for no apparent reason, any endeavor or relationship we build can be haphazardly destroyed? This unfair philosophy would have you believe that we're all strolling along through a beautiful world that also happens to be a giant, inescapable minefield.

The Truth:

As humans, we all have the capacity to broaden our perceptions of life into greater and greater awareness. Animals are at a disadvantage in the awareness game. For example, *"Life is fair"* isn't the first thought on a gazelle's mind as it runs flat-out with a cheetah in hot pursuit. But as far as we can tell, gazelles don't spend much time contemplating the "why" behind life events. They're solely focused on survival.

The simple, beautiful truth is that life is inherently fair. The catch is that most of us were never taught to perceive this truth. Enhanced perception of higher truth doesn't typically happen on its own. One must be humble and open enough to notice that there's much more to life than meets the eye (or that meets any of our physical senses). Once we broaden our attention beyond the physical aspect of life, we'll become aware of an intelligence that's too big and too profound to be explained. This intelligence is something that we're all equally part of. When we finally feel it, it becomes a comforting warmth that can get us through our darkest days and burn through life's painful delusions.

The Solution:

One way to navigate around the lie of unfairness is to consider the idea that "unfair" is a short-term judgment that's disconnected from long-term outcomes. And by long-term, I'm referring to the soul's perspective of long-term, not the body's perspective. Our soul is who we really are. But the soul can easily get lost in fiction while it's using the tools of our mind and our body to craft our life story. There's no getting around this: As long as you believe that you are only your mind and body, you will likely be pulled into believing that life is unfair. This time-limited perspective creates frustration, fear, and confusion, and it keeps you stuck in the short-term - with a meager one hundred years or so as your only outlook and frame of reference. As a result, tragedy, suffering, and pain will be experienced as senseless absolutes instead of doorways to greater meaning, higher purpose, and larger stories.

While our concept of fairness eventually evolves as our awareness expands, we must work with what we currently perceive as fair and unfair. It reflects well on us, for example, when we stand up for those who are wrongfully

5

persecuted. But it's when we're open to seeing higher purpose in the entire life process - in the offenses of others as well as our responses to them - that we can begin to dismantle the concept of unfairness itself. This big picture perspective is a very high bar to reach. However, any lofty spiritual or philosophical realizations we achieve in no way change the truth that when we act selflessly in support of others, we create a better world.

To pursue deeper wisdom on this topic, you can't let *"Life isn't fair"* stop at your thoughts. Try to *feel* past the concept of unfairness. Decide there must be something you're missing: an obscured truth about yourself or about life that points to a more complex reality; something printed between the lines of your story and the stories of others; something hiding in plain sight waiting to be deciphered. If you're earnestly open to that type of discovery, what once appeared as a jumbled mess of painful circumstances will begin to make sense to you. The price of this clarity is that you let go - just for a moment - of your assumptions about how life works. When you do that, a door will automatically open to new insights that are beyond your intellect. This is when the concept of unfairness starts to fall apart, and a spectacular matrix of spiritual evolution reveals itself.

The sum of anyone's life is a never-ending story of long-game fairness, progress, and growth that reconciles itself throughout eternity. The seemingly unfair difficulties we encounter will eventually be understood as vital pieces of our soul's journey that we didn't realize we needed. If anything in life ever appears to you as unfair, you either can't see the whole story yet, or your definition of life isn't nearly big enough.

LIE #2: I AM ALONE

The Deception:

There are many people, even those who live with others, who experience heavy inner isolation. Yet their belief that they are alone is not an intuitive feeling; it's a constructed thought that is fundamentally mistaken. Being alone does not cause the emotion of loneliness. It's the fear that one is neglected and will always be alone - whether physically or emotionally - that leads us to feeling sad. In life, our thoughts are the genesis behind how we experience reality. As long as your thoughts are of the self-centered, *"Why isn't anyone paying attention to me?"* variety, your world will look like a lonely place. This loneliness originates in your mind, and from there, it gets projected into your life. Ultimately, reality is what we make of it. And one way to make something new out of our present reality is to change our thinking about it.

Throughout the course of our lives, most of us have experienced a sense of loneliness. But there isn't a single person who hasn't also experienced some form of joyful connection. Human connectedness always exists some-where in our world. And because we're part of this world, feeling connected is always possible for us. Noticing this constant opportunity will turn loneliness into a mirage that disappears as soon as we investigate it.

The Truth:

To fully uncover the loneliness lie, it helps to begin with a bigger picture. Leading astrophysicists have determined that within our Milky Way galaxy, there are potentially tens of millions of worlds capable of sustaining life. That's tens of millions of chances - just in our galaxy - that we're not alone (setting aside that there're *billions* of galaxies out there). By running the numbers, it becomes very hard to believe that life exists only on our tiny world and nowhere else in the Universe.

Getting back down to Earth... every one of us is in companionship with all life on this planet. "Mother Earth," after all, is what we're made of (at least physically). All you need to do to perceive this is water a plant, feed some ducks, or look deeply into a dog's eyes. If you're paying close attention, you will instantly feel a connection. Beyond our animal friends, of course, you're living here with several billion of your own species. That's billions of human souls who share so many of your experiences - from basic ones like losing baby teeth, the awkwardness of puberty, and the responsibilities of being an adult - to more advanced experiences, like contemplating life and death, being inspired by a touching story, or falling in love.

The truth is, you couldn't be alone in this world if you tried. We're all irreversibly partnered with each other - not only because we share so many things in common, but because it takes all of us working together to make life function. Despite our differences, humanity is indeed a family. Connecting to this truth exposes loneliness as the paper tiger that it is.

The Solution:

One of the fastest ways to defeat a lonely thought is to flip the script on your inward thinking. Turn your attention outward instead. Give others what it is you want to receive. Ask yourself if you know anyone at this moment who might be thinking they're alone. Then, ponder what you can do to help them understand that they're mistaken. This could be as simple as a brief text to just say hi, or maybe putting their birthday on your calendar as a reminder to reach out to them that day. But don't stop at only the people you know; go out of your way to smile at a stranger while walking down the street. Always look behind you when opening a door to see if there's someone close enough who'd appreciate you holding it open. Let others into traffic whenever you can, and don't forget to wave thanks at those who let you in. All these seemingly small things are points of connection that actively ground you in the truth that you are not alone. And the more you do these kinds of things, the more your focus will be outward and expansive instead of inward and isolating. With this simple approach of placing a higher value on human interaction, relationships will blossom, and loneliness will fade.

A joyful, connected future is waiting for you at this very moment, and there's relatively little work that needs to be done to achieve it. So many people stand to benefit from even a brief encounter with anyone who gets up in the morning wanting to connect to the world. And it's often the small things we do for each other that enrich our lives and make the world kinder. Everyone has something heartfelt to give and something heartwarming to receive. And it's this constant exchange that feeds our collective souls and makes life worth living.

Life is much bigger than you think it is, and you've only explored a small part of it. If you truly open your heart to this world and sincerely desire to connect with it, a tsunami of kinship that washes away loneliness will come rushing in.

LIE #3: I'M NOT SMART ENOUGH

The Deception:

The rickety structure of this lie is anchored in the belief that somebody messed up. You're not supposed to be here... the chromosomes that resulted in your birth were a bad combination... or some forgetful deity was slacking on the day you were born when they were supposed to equip you with what you needed. Take your pick of whatever fabricated nonsense about inadequacy speaks to you most. But understand that you're not alone in thinking this way. Self-doubt is a rite of passage. And whether we admit it or not, we've all had it.

The issue here is humanity's insidious tendency to compare. Comparison is a misguided attempt to orient ourselves in this big world while trying to figure out who we are and where we fit in. What we look like, how athletic we are, how high we score on tests, what goals we set, how successful we are at accomplishing those goals... all or any of this can become a comparative, self-destructive obsession.

Yet it's our individual differences and variety of expression that should be celebrated. If we aren't careful, though (and many of us aren't), this celebration of natural, wonderful diversity quickly devolves into a brutally competitive, hierarchical culture of "better than."

The Truth:

You are here. And regardless of what anyone - even your parents - may have told you, your being here is no accident. Life found an important expression through you, and nothing was powerful enough to stop that expression from manifesting into the person you are. Call it whatever you want - God, your Higher Self, the Universal Oneness, or some cosmic video game designer who created your character - you are part of an immense, cooperative system of life, and you positively have a role in that system. Obviously, no two roles can be the same. But it's intensely distracting to see another's role that you perceive to be better than yours because they can do things you can't. And there's the problem: While you're looking around comparing yourself to others, you lose sight of the amazing things that are part of you.

Everyone on this planet, despite any perceived disadvantages, has something unique and exceptional to offer. There are endless examples of this truth: individuals with mental and physical disabilities who've completed triathlons; writers and filmmakers who were rejected again and again to later become leaders in their fields; and everyday people who overcome addiction, trauma, or depression and go on to live fulfilling lives that benefit others. Each of us is immensely more than the aggregate of our genetics. We came into this life - along with all our characteristics - for the benefit of life itself.

The Solution:

To dispel this false idea that you don't have enough intelligence or talent in life, look to your passion. Everyone has one. And if you think you don't, that just means you haven't uncovered it yet. Reflect on what interests you, inspires you, moves you, excites you, or pulls you in. Look to see what you gladly spend your time doing. What activity or engagement makes time fly by for you? Don't fall into the trap of filtering your passions through others' judgments and expectations. As long as you're doing no harm to yourself or others, ignore your critics.

Once you connect with your passion, hold on to it tightly. It sounds cliché, but belief is the main engine behind any venture, and courage is the ignition for that engine. When you find an endeavor that brings you joy - however insignificant you think that endeavor might be - leaping into it is what energizes and activates the undiscovered talent and intelligence within you. We're all smarter and more talented than we know, and our passion is the guidance that leads to untold treasures hidden within each one of us.

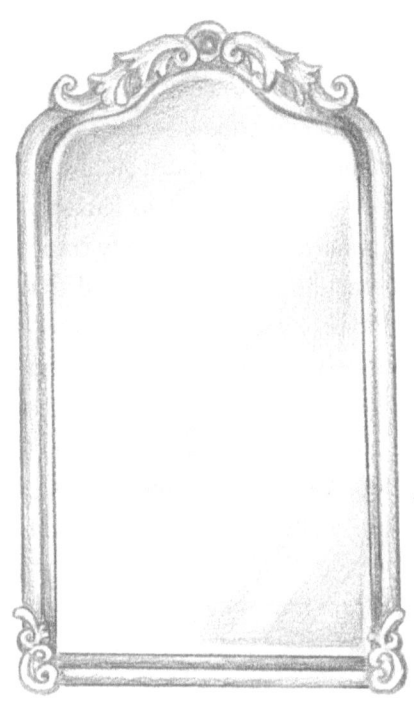

LIE #4: I'M NOT ATTRACTIVE ENOUGH

The Deception:

The blobfish is widely regarded as one of the ugliest living things on Earth. This lethargic animal has very little muscle mass and hardly any bones. But because blobfish live thousands of feet beneath the ocean, their gelatinous anatomy is perfectly adapted to survive the immense pressure at those extreme depths. When brought to the surface, a blobfish looks to us like a hideous, melting mess of a creature that's having a very bad day (these fish actually frown). Although, if you could ask a blobfish to describe its ideal picture of attractiveness, it would describe... another blobfish (which, of course, is why there're always more blobfish).

The point of this example is to illustrate that there's no universal standard for beauty. Every creature, as well as every human, has inherent beauty. And that beauty isn't dependent upon how widely it's recognized. In the wilderness, attractiveness based on physical characteristics is king. During mating season, the biggest, strongest, or most colorful tend to dominate the gene pool. Attractiveness in human society, though, is more than just skin (or scale) deep. Thankfully, many of us have achieved a higher "attraction perspective" that makes it difficult to separate how a person looks from how they act.

The Truth:

It doesn't matter what you look like. Despite whatever so-called deformity you have or whichever ways your face or body don't comply with society's shallow norms of beauty, you are beautiful. Full stop. If you can't see this, you're not looking hard enough. This book is not religious, but it's helpful here to quote the age-old advice to *"See yourself through the eyes of God."* There's a good reason this phrase has been tossed around for millennia. Taken literally or figuratively, it invites us to shift our self-view by looking deeper into ourselves. This means looking beneath the superficial, animalistic perspective of beauty to find our true beauty... our soul's beauty. And once we discover it, that beauty more freely animates all aspects of our life and our being. When you begin to appreciate your own inner and outer beauty, the dark cloud of insecurity that follows you around is lifted, and you automatically glow and shine in so many new ways.

For reasons that might be temporarily beyond your awareness, the way you look is perfectly suited to the life you're living right now. You've been given the perfect "equipment" to get the most out of this lifetime while experiencing what you came here to experience. Whether your physical form is rough around the edges (like a rugged, off-road vehicle) or sleek and precise (like a Formula 1 race car), the body you have is exactly what you need. And part of the wonder of life is discovering and understanding how your physical appearance fits perfectly into your personal mission of learning, growing, and creating happiness.

The Solution:

From everyday Fords to exotic Ferraris, as well as anything in between, all cars look better when they're well taken care of. There's a fine line to walk, however, regarding physical self-improvement. We must be careful that when we "improve" our bodies, we're doing it for ourselves and not to fit someone else's idea of how we should look. Having said that, there are basic maintenance practices that not only enhance our appearance but also enhance our physical and mental health. For example, maybe your doctor has fired a warning shot across your hood ornament by suggesting a beneficial change in diet and exercise habits.

Maybe you've decided on your own to lose some weight, and you know that doing so would make you feel better. Or maybe you think you'd look better if you'd comb your hair more often... or less often. What matters most is your personal motivation. As long as that motivation isn't being controlled by someone or something external, and you're reaching for a version of your physical self that inspires you, you're most likely on the right track.

Remember, your beauty shines brightest when you're not trying to be someone else's idea of beautiful, but when you're expressing your beauty in your own way. And above all, don't wait for others to see the beauty in you before you see it in yourself.

LIE #5: MY BEST ISN'T GOOD ENOUGH

The Deception:

Whether we're working at our job, parenting children, or playing games with friends, we all want to be good at what we're doing. Playfully or professionally, this desire is reinforced by our co-workers, our kids, and our friends wanting us to excel and "not let them down." Within healthy parameters, that kind of work / family / social dynamic is what drives our growth as human beings. There's absolutely no problem with wanting to improve ourselves by being a better employee, manager, parent, or friend. But when it comes to excelling, problems crop up quickly when we forget that we're not robots.

From the moment a simple machine is switched on for the first time, it starts doing exactly what it was designed to do. There's no learning curve for a hairdryer; it gets the job done right on day one and every day thereafter until it eventually burns out. We have a job to do and a role to play, just like the hairdryer. But "getting it right" looks much different for us than it does for a machine because our "getting it right" usually includes a bit of getting it wrong. Unlike a hairdryer's job, which never changes, our jobs as human beings change all the time. Each day brings a new set of circumstances, interactions, and personal challenges that we must creatively adjust to. Thus, we discover that "getting it right" isn't supposed to be an obsession with perfection. It's simply a game of not giving up after we get it wrong.

The Truth:

When I was younger, I was an instructor at a high-performance driving school. After all the classroom instruction, the last thing we'd tell our beginner students before taking them on the racetrack for the first time was, *"Remember... keep the shiny side up!"* This comment, which was another way of saying, "Don't wreck," usually elicited a chuckle from our students, but it was actually a crucial reminder that the most important aspect of driving is safety. Going fast can be fun, but if safety is neglected, that fun can disappear in an instant. Doing your best while safely driving down the metaphorical road of life is very similar. If you become so focused on fast-paced achievement that you start to neglect yourself, you'll eventually spin out of control - physically, emotionally, or both.

Not only is your best effort good enough in life, but less than your best is also good enough. Demanding from ourselves - or from anyone else - the absolute best outcome 100% of the time is a recipe for anxiety, depression, poor health, and an eventual psychological meltdown. Whatever gains you've made in a suffocating, high-pressure atmosphere of perfection can be erased very quickly, for example, with an extended hospital stay or a run-in with substance abuse.

To be clear, this isn't an assault on doing your best. This train of thought merely suggests that sometimes, for whatever reason, your best might not be accessible. Maybe you didn't sleep well or aren't feeling well… maybe you've got personal or relationship issues on your mind… or maybe the task at hand isn't something that interests or inspires you. On any given day, you can only muster what you've got to muster with. But day after day, if you make a habit of simply showing up and giving whatever it is you've got to give, that'll be enough.

The Solution:

It may seem paradoxical and somewhat ironic, but the key to doing your best and "getting it right" depends on your capacity to let go of outcomes. Lao Tzu, the author of the *Tao Te Ching* (one of history's greatest philosophical texts), figured this out about 2,500 years ago. This venerable Chinese philosopher made clear that he's a big fan of putting forth a solid effort to accomplish a goal. After we make that effort, though, Lao Tzu cautions us about attachment to results. Much of his work has a central theme of achieving peace of mind. He illustrates that the enemy of inner peace is emotionally tying yourself to results over which you have no control. Not only is a preoccupation with future outcomes energetically wasteful, he argues, but the worry it causes distracts you from your efforts in the present moment. Whatever happens in the future does not affect the quality of the effort you've already given. That effort stands in noble independence from its result. If Lao Tzu were around today, I feel he'd offer us this simple mantra for maintaining inner peace in our lives: *Give it a go, and then let it go.*

As life peppers us with its timeless wisdom by way of our experiences, we'll all eventually discover an elegantly simple tactic for doing our best: *Be present and live in the now.* When we refuse to live in the scary, imaginary future that our minds often take us to, we'll find a majestic inner peace in the present moment that automatically makes our best *better*. From there, we can accept whatever outcome our efforts yield, and we'll understand that getting it wrong is sometimes an important part of getting it right.

LIE #6: I'M NOT STRONG ENOUGH

The Deception:

We've all had feelings of weakness. Trivially, we may feel a little weak when we yield to the urge for an unhealthy midnight snack... or when we're outfoxed by our inner procrastinator that repeatedly makes a case for skipping exercise... or even sometimes when we fall to the formidable force that is the snooze button on our morning alarm. More intensely, awful feelings of weakness and resignation can visit us... sometimes after a painful relationship breakup... or in the wake of losing a job... and certainly in the aftermath of a loved one's passing. Being hit by forces like these is sometimes part of life. Inherent within us all, however, is the strength to deal with anything life can throw at us. When we find that strength within, this doesn't mean we'll suddenly experience life as a continual walk in the park. But the very act of trying to be strong - or even looking for our strength - is self-inspiring and causes strength we never knew we had to surface.

We can, though, be deceived by our own experiences. It's easy to remember times we felt weak, just as it's easy to remember times we felt strong. But a common mistake is assuming that the weak experiences we've had represent who we are, and that the strong experiences we've had are as strong as we'll ever be. Let's clear this up. You are not your weaknesses. And no matter how strong you think you are, the strength you've experienced is only a fraction of the strength you've yet to discover within.

The Truth:

No one is born stronger or weaker than another. Cutting through the façade of physicality, our souls all share the same metaphysical DNA of extraordinary strength. But no two souls are having the same "strength experience" at the same time. This, then, creates the illusion of one person being stronger or weaker than another, kind of like a Kodiak bear cub not being as strong as its 1,400-pound, full-grown father. Both bears have the same physical DNA for strength and therefore the same potential. But real strength - otherwise known as spiritual strength - is called into action when life becomes difficult. And it's those difficult times that serve as the main catalyst for growing into a stronger version of ourselves.

When you feel weak, it's not because you are weak. In those moments, life is trying to coax you into seeing - and thereby experiencing - your difficult circumstances from a higher perspective. Anyone you look up to as being a person of strength has at some point along their journey felt that they weren't strong enough. And through the highs and lows of that journey, they didn't take a pill to suddenly become strong; they elevated their perspective about their circumstances, allowing them to engage those circumstances in different, more effective ways. That pivot of perspective is what we see as strength.

Being strong is not about having strength for strength's sake. The real reason for finding our strength is that it allows us to help others, and in so doing, experience much higher joys in life than we thought possible. As we climb the ladder of life experiences, we'll find that there's no ceiling to the joy we can access. And that joy, when bolstered by compassion for others, eventually becomes less and less dependent on circumstances.

The Solution:

Whenever you feel that you're not strong enough, tell yourself that it's okay to feel that way. When a child is afraid of the dark, it's okay for them to feel that way, too. Try to see yourself in those vulnerable moments as the child who - for the time being - needs a nightlight. Remember, though, that no one remains a child forever. And the fear or weakness you feel are necessary steps along the way to mental and spiritual adulthood. Children don't grow up overnight, and adults who have climbed their way to a summit of strength didn't leap there in a single bound. But when you're down and you feel that you need a pity party, go ahead and throw one for yourself. Start by saying out loud what your fear wants to say. Don't muffle that voice. Let it shout out its negative, shortsighted conclusions. If you let it speak freely, you'll more easily see it as a false voice that doesn't represent you or your life's true potential.

As you know, you're not the only one going through internal tugs-of-war like this. When you understand that your feelings of weakness are merely innocent, childlike confusion, you'll have greater patience with those in your life who also struggle with occasional delusions of weakness. This is a universal experience. And when someone doesn't show up as strong as you want them to, remember that they - like the rest of us - are in life's inescapable strength training program. Life isn't trying to break us; it's trying to help us. And at every turn and with every challenge, life is attempting to show us how strong we are.

LIE #7: I HAVE TO KEEP UP

The Deception:

In the roughly 5,000 years that humanity has kept records, life has never changed so rapidly as it has over the past 100 years. We now live in a world where technology is advancing exponentially. A mere 68 years after the Wright brothers' historic first flight, humanity put a space station into orbit. Today, a bargain-priced calculator casually thrown into an 8th grader's backpack has hundreds of times more computing power than the 1969 Apollo moon lander. And a typical phone nowadays is more than a million times more powerful than that moon lander's computer. From self-driving cars and autonomous drones to artificial intelligence systems that can just about read your mind, life in the 21st century is like living aboard a high-tech express, and it's most certainly a runaway train.

Amid this technological tumult, many - especially those who are no longer considered "young" - can sometimes feel out of touch, helpless, or even obsolete. For them, the rules of life keep changing, and the memos about those changes seem to reach them later and later or not at all. To add insult to injury, cultural evolution is also progressing at a frenetic pace. Trends in music, film, fashion, and even language can pass us by if we aren't paying close attention. As we get older, it can feel as though we're running in slow motion while the world around us is set to fast-forward. In today's tempest of transformation, the net takeaway is often a very fearful, *"If I don't keep up, I'll be left behind!"* But if a crazy train left you behind, should you really be that concerned?

The Truth:

To care, or not to care - that is the question. Or, more to the point, what is it that you do care about? For instance, do you really care about incessantly commenting on social media - even ignoring people in your physical presence to do so? Or do you care more about spending uninterrupted time with friends and loved ones in ways that don't involve a digital interface? In our screen-addicted world, the desire for quantity of interaction has regrettably surpassed the desire for quality of interaction. Is this detached and arguably unhealthy new norm of "connecting" worth keeping up with? A significant portion of today's apps in the digital arena are making millions of people secretly depressed. Envy and self-judgment arise when we look through deceivingly filtered social media lenses into others' lives. Over-indulging in social platforms does not enrich us; rather, it distracts us from that which authentically enriches us.

The intent here is not to wage war against the technological progress and achievements of humanity. There are many new and wonderful innovations - including digital connections with others - that truly do enhance our lives. But too much of a good thing very quickly becomes a bad thing. And the truth is that our biggest opportunity to "keep up" is to keep ourselves in a healthy balance with technology instead of being addictively reliant upon it. How well you keep up with technology is not a valid measure for self-worth, nor is it a valid measure of the benefit you are and can be to others. Who you are is immeasurably more important than how well you're connected. Living a life of compassion and integrity means infinitely more than how many followers you have or how quickly you respond to instant messages.

The Solution:

It's important to note that not everyone needs to play by the same rules when it comes to keeping up. One

27

person's balanced approach to technology is another person's technological and social starvation. One size does not fit all. But it's prudent to have a sense of self-awareness that serves as an internal barometer for how much is too much. For example, if you can't exercise, have a meal with a friend, watch a show, or even use the bathroom without habitually checking your phone, it's likely you're out of balance. The solution is to catch yourself behaving as an unconscious slave to your screen, and then taking action to moderate yourself. This may be as simple as adjusting your phone settings during lunch with a friend so that only critical contacts (like your spouse or your child's school) can get through to you. Self-moderation can also look like resisting the urge to check your messages if you happen to wake up in the middle of the night.

Swimming against this obsessive social current may be uncomfortable at times, but your mental health will greatly benefit from doing so. Setting parameters for yourself as well as others, and then consciously holding to those parameters, is the key to finding your unique blueprint for balance.

If you still find yourself fretting about keeping up with the digital world, remember that life is ultimately about keeping up with just one thing: increasing the love and compassion you have for yourself and for others. That daily, internal "software update" equips you with everything you really need in life. All good things - including balance - will flow from that one, kindhearted endeavor.

LIE #8: I COULD NEVER BE AS GOOD AS THEY ARE

The Deception:

Whether it's gorillas pounding their chests, dictators parading missiles down main street, or players trash-talking each other on a sports field, intimidation has long been the primary tool for showing dominance in both the literal and metaphorical jungles of our world. Frequently, even in the absence of another's intimidation tactics, we talk ourselves into being intimidated. The moment we see another person doing what we do for work, playing our sport, singing our song, or whatever, the potential exists for us to default into a kind of animalistic, fight-or-flight reaction. As mentioned earlier, this is rooted in our tendency to compare ourselves to others while trying to understand where we rank in a competitive hierarchy. A subtle insecurity often creeps into our minds if we're unsure of who we're better than and who's better than we are. This would serve us well if we were animals in an actual jungle. But as human beings, we have a choice to silence that paranoid instinct while evolving beyond a Darwinian, survival of the fittest mentality.

When it comes to excelling, our minds are usually the biggest obstacle to surmount before we achieve anything. And a mind that's intimidated by its surroundings will be continually stuck in an *"I can't do it"* mentality. To break out of this negativity, it's necessary to see through the lie that someone else's success somehow raises the bar beyond our ability to achieve.

The Truth:

When you say that you could never be as good as some-one else at something, you're right. That is, on your own, you're right. No one accomplishes anything in this world completely on their own. The support that helped them achieve whatever they achieved may not be visible, but rest assured, it was there. Mentors, parents, teachers, friends, heroes, divine inspirations, or even a brief but impactful encounter with a stranger can significantly alter someone's life trajectory. Though we don't always see it, our world is a vast, interdependent web of life. It doesn't matter what degree of hardship life has dealt us; it's impossible to be in this world and not be supported by it in some way.

Sometimes it will seem like the world is doing the exact opposite of supporting you. But a stretch of what may ap-pear to you as "bad luck" always hides significant meaning and purpose within it. Life itself conspires to give you never-ending opportunities to improve yourself as well as your circumstances. Improvement means that you're taking the raw material of something that's less than ideal and making something better out of it. The truth is that all the support you could ever need to improve yourself and your life is out there. When you're sincerely open to receiving help, that support will be much easier to find. And in many cases, it will find you.

The Solution:

In any field or endeavor, there are countless stories of those who've defied the odds and achieved what was thought to be unachievable. The people in those stories are not superhuman - they're just like you and me. They had a path to success which they followed one step at a time. The basic mechanics of those success stories are no different than the basic mechanics of anyone's life. Whether it's destitution to vast wealth or unspeakable trauma to ecstatic happiness, any negative extreme you can think of has at some time been overcome and transformed. And it's all happened with the assistance of many helping hands. So, when you see those successful people, try not to believe the lie that you could never do what they did or be as good as they are. Think instead, *"With life's built-in support, 'we' can be as good as they are."* Choosing thoughts like this brings you into immediate resonance with your own personal cavalry that's always been standing by, just out of sight. What separates you most from that cavalry of support is your own disbelief.

A word of caution: Before crusading off on an endeavor to be as good as someone else at something, it's essential to examine your motivation for doing so. Run a self-diagnostic to make sure your ego isn't trying to take you in one direction while your heart wants to take you in another. Thoroughly dig into what's driving you toward your goal and root out any trace of wanting to impress others or gain their approval. Anything built on a foundation of self-glorification will eventually collapse on itself. To navigate around this ego trap, remember that authenticity of self is the master key to lasting self-improvement and happiness. Don't focus on how you want the world to see you; focus instead on how you want to see yourself. Then at last, the no-win scenario of trying to live up to someone else's expectation ends, and the sweet song of being in harmony with your true self begins.

LIE #9: I CAN'T CHANGE

The Deception:

Let's get the obvious part of this lie out of the way: No society, trend, culture, government, friend, or family group should be in control of who you are. If you've consciously or unconsciously granted any of them this authority, revoke it immediately. Despite societal pressures or judgments from people close to you, you're the only one who should be deciding how you live your life. Once you have a firm grip on that personal precept, only then is it time to contemplate ways that you'd like to change.

Having disabled the external world's manipulative control over you, your next mission is to confront your inner world. When you begin to consider changing how you think and act, get ready for a picket line of protesting thoughts that will loudly parade around inside your head. These naysayers (your own doubts and fears manifested in self-talk) will be yelling things like, "*You can't escape your conditioning and your genetics!*" "*You're too old to change!*" "*It's not worth the effort!*" "*You failed before, and you'll fail again!*" The volume and repetition of these negative thoughts can be overwhelming, and they can easily overtake you... unless you really want to change.

A well-known parable about a Zen Master speaks to the process of creating consequential change in one's life. One day, the master was meditating by a river when a young, spiritual aspirant approached him. *"Master, I am ready to pursue the path of enlightenment. Please show me the way."* The master responded, *"Are you certain you want to walk the way of enlightenment and that you want it more than anything?"* *"Yes,"* the young aspirant replied. *"Then follow me to the river."* And with that, he followed the master into waist-deep water. The master then gripped the back of the young man's neck and forcefully shoved his face underwater. More than a little startled, the aspirant struggled to lift his head from the water, but the master held it firmly beneath the surface. Nearly out of air and beginning to panic, the young man broke the master's firm grip by heaving his head out of the river with all his might, taking in a huge, gasping breath. *"Why did you do that?!!"* the exasperated young man shrieked. The master calmly replied, *"You asked me to show you the way. When you want enlightenment as much as you wanted that breath, only then are you ready to begin."*

The Truth:

In the parable of the Zen Master and the spiritual aspirant, the word "enlightenment" can easily be swapped for the word "change." Anyone is capable of change, but not everyone is motivated to change. It's the idea and vision of how much better life could be that eventually becomes the inspiration for change. Although, initially, a state of desperation can also be a powerful motivator. A pitfall for employing change is when we realize what must be done or given up to make change happen. It's at this point that many people default into their comfort zone, becoming numb to their aspirations of improving themselves and their lives. In sailing, this is called being "in irons," a state where a vessel's progress stops as its sails flap in the wind. To get "out of irons," the boat's sails must be trimmed so they can catch the wind again. When we've lost our wind in life, we usually need a little help to get it back. But with a bit of self-observation, we'll recognize that life offers all the help we need at every turn (or in sailing parlance, at every tack).

Life's assistance is elegantly simple and ever-present. When we experience harmony in life, this tells us that what we're doing is working and that change - at least for now - isn't necessary. When we experience disharmony in life - in our relationships, in our work life, or in our physical or mental health - it means that what we're doing isn't working, and it's time to change something. If we ignore disharmony, it inevitably amplifies, and eventually, any "comfort zone numbness" we've found will turn into an intolerable ache. This is how life speaks to us, guides us, and nudges us into the changes that are necessary for us to grow and experience greater joy.

The Solution:

The solution for seeing through the lie of *"I can't change"* boils down to two words: vision and persistence. Having vision means taking the time to make two assessments: 1) Where do you want to go; and 2) Where are you currently heading? When you do the math, the difference between those two answers will be obvious, and that's when your motivation to change can kick in. If you're genuinely in touch with your heart, you'll be inspired by the possibilities that change would bring, or you'll be disturbed by the imagined future that not changing would bring. Either way, you've got your motivation.

Regarding persistence, gardening teaches us all we need to know about this subject. To have a beautiful or productive garden, removing weeds that sap nutrients and block sunlight is a necessity. And obviously, this isn't something that's done only once. Weeding and gardening are inseparable just as change and persistence are inseparable. You can't expect change to yield anything if you change for a little while and then go back to the way you were or to what you were doing before. Change isn't a part-time endeavor; it's a commitment to become something different or transform what you're doing into something new. When you do this, life - along with everyone and everything in it - will change in response. Because life is interactive, it has no choice in this. Realize also that doubt and fear are part of change as well. If you feel them, then you know you're really changing and not just trying to convince yourself that you're changing. In those moments when fear grips you, as it likely will when you change something, remember to hold on to your inspiring vision, and breathe... deeply and slowly. Simple, mindful breathing will help the fear pass and allow change to proceed.

LIE #10: I WAS TOO DAMAGED AS A CHILD

The Deception:

This is one of the tougher lies. Negative impressions and experiences - especially traumatic ones - which occurred during our youth, can become dark filters through which we view ourselves and the world. Unless these filters are removed, they can negatively color our entire life experience. The key to removing the "damaged as a child" filter is understanding the misperceptions that hold that filter in place. If you believe that something or someone from your childhood irreversibly damaged you, then that will be your experience for as long as you believe that painful lie.

It's important to highlight that any trauma or difficulty you may have experienced as a child should not be disregarded or suppressed. As children, most of us lacked the resources and maturity required to fully process emotionally difficult experiences. As adults, it's critical to seek out whatever help is necessary to work through any psychological hurdles from childhood. But it would be a mistake to begin that process under the assumption that some scars can't be healed or that what you went through cannot eventually be overcome.

The Truth:

Thinking that you are damaged beyond repair is believing that who you are can be altered or created by another. While your physical body is created through a biological process, what's under the hood, so to speak, isn't something anyone else but you has the power to permanently change. You can be temporarily convinced that past experiences have made you inferior, but that delusion is blind to the absolute reality of the unalterable qualities you possess within.

To grasp this truth, imagine driving a car through an intense storm. As you struggle to keep the car on the road, hurricane force winds buffet the vehicle, torrential rain blinds your view, and golf ball-size hail smashes into your windshield and headlights. Your car has taken quite a beating. But although you're shaken, you emerge from that car the same person you were before the storm (albeit, more experienced). Just because you went through a storm doesn't fundamentally change the person you are deep inside. And although your car (or metaphorically, your life) appears damaged, you, as the driver, remain intact. Comprehending this means that not only will you be ready to hit the road again, you'll be a much better driver as a result.

The Solution:

It's difficult to provide a lasting solution to this lie without the aid of a spiritual perspective. If you don't yet know yourself as something more than your mental and physical self, the delusion of being damaged or inferior will likely come back at some point. To fully demolish this lie, you must understand that you are bigger than that lie. Gaining this understanding requires humility. Admit that you don't have all the answers to who you are or why you're here. This admission helps disable any inflexible, default perspective you might have of *"If I can't see it or prove it, it doesn't exist."* Most major discoveries in modern science at first couldn't be seen or proved... until they were. The same holds true for a higher part of you - a part that's beyond your intellect and physicality. That's the part that can't be damaged or destroyed. And once that part is rediscovered, it has the capacity to heal all the other parts of you.

Embracing yourself as something beyond what your mind can perceive goes a long way in dispelling the *"I was damaged"* lie. But to go all the way, you must remove this lie's last remaining source of fuel: the past. When you decide that the present moment and your present life are much more important than any past moments of your life, you're no longer within this lie's reach. You've stopped fixating on the past, and you have moved on. That kind of letting go and looking forward is extremely healing. However, one indispensable part of true healing is working toward forgiving whoever was involved in your childhood trauma, or for that matter, whoever's associated with any difficulties from your past. Letting go of the past cannot be done without forgiveness. But more on that later...

LIE #11: I'M NOT MEANT FOR LOVE

The Deception:

"No one wants me." "I'm not compatible with anyone." "It's too late for love in my life." These are just a few of the thoughts that can cross a lovelorn mind. Anyone who has an unfulfilled desire to meet a life partner, and certainly anyone who's experienced a rough breakup, has likely gone through a period of hopeless frustration. This vortex

of sorrow typically begins externally; i.e., *"There's no one out there for me."* And if enough time passes without partnering success, one can easily descend into thoughts like, *"It's me, not them... I must not be datable."* We need to pause here, because whether we're talking about one's dating life or life in general, asking ourselves tough questions about our circumstances and seeking objective answers is a healthy process. Yes, there may be things that you're doing or not doing, which can adversely affect your dating life. These things you can change, if you feel so compelled. But it's a lie to believe that you are not meant for love and are inherently defective when it comes to relationships. That's like trying to eat soup with the wrong end of a spoon and believing it's the spoon that's defective and not how you're using it.

The Truth:

For all those who desire a life partner, there is someone out there for them. No one is a freak. No matter how extreme, tragic, dark, or strange your life experiences have been, rest assured there's someone else who's been through something similar and can potentially understand you. We live in a big world. Even in the smallest towns and villages, it's possible to meet a newcomer... to meet someone passing through... or to meet in a new way someone you thought you knew but didn't really (perhaps even rekindling an old flame). And in this age of digital connectivity, meeting someone virtually has become a viable and effective way to expand one's scope of possibilities. The point is, whatever small sample of the dating pool you've experienced thus far, there are still countless, wonderful personalities that you've yet to encounter. And like a scientist in a lab, you have no idea how your chemistry will react with others' chemistry. It's an exciting adventure to see what aspects of your character are highlighted and enhanced by different potential partners.

Disclaimer: Chemistry is a field of experimentation. And sometimes experiments can blow up in one's face. That's what safety glasses are for. But in the dating arena, it's important not to be afraid of failed experiments. You begin by wearing your metaphorical lab coat and glasses in the form of managed expectations and healthy boundaries. These precautions are prudent whether you're in a new relationship or attempting to revitalize an old one. In any case, each time you have a mishap in the lab of your love life, take note of what worked and what didn't work, clean up the mess as best you can, and move on to the next experiment. In the process, you'll learn something new about relationships, and just as important, you'll likely learn something new about yourself.

The Solution:

Since antiquity, sages in India have taught of the pursuit of enlightenment using a metaphorical story about a wife whose husband has left home to fight in a great battle. The wife doesn't know when or even if her husband will return. Yet each day she prepares the house and herself as if that day is the day of his arrival. She certainly has the option to sit around sulking because her beloved husband isn't with her. But instead, she takes joy in beautifying her home and herself so that she's always ready to receive him. The point of this story as taught in ashrams and monasteries is to never be slack in your spiritual practice and commitment, because enlightenment (a.k.a., your beloved) could come to you at any time, and it's your constant preparation that elicits and enhances this arrival.

This spiritual teaching story is easily adapted to dating. Ask yourself, *"In what ways can I make myself ready for love?"* This is a complex question that has as many different answers as there are people. But a good place to start is by reflecting on what it is you're looking for in someone else and then considering how you can enhance those same qualities within yourself. For example, if you happen to admire the qualities of patience, spontaneity, and fitness, then read a book about patience, do things occasionally without planning them, and adopt an exercise routine. When you accentuate aspects within yourself that you admire, you develop a resonance with those who are accentuating those same aspects within themselves. In doing so, you remain ever ready for that unexpected encounter and for your "beloved" to finally come home.

LIE #12: I NEED SOMEONE TO COMPLETE ME

The Deception:

From romance novels to romantic comedies, there's no shortage of societal forces trying to convince us that we're incomplete and need someone else to complete us. From one angle, this can be a very alluring prospect. It puts the seemingly complex and daunting task of finding happiness squarely on the shoulders of another. If we could just find the right partner, we would avoid all the heavy lifting of having to figure out happiness on our own, right? No, not quite. While it's true that souls who resonate deeply with each other and choose to spend their lives together share one of the highest joys life can offer, that scenario is not a prerequisite for fulfillment or happiness.

The Truth:

We may desperately want an intimate partner, but no matter how perfect that partner may be for us, they will be incapable of giving to us that which we deny ourselves. Life is difficult. And there are potentially depressing, confus-ing, and scary spectacles wherever we look. But alongside that, there is endless beauty, goodness, and compassion in life, which translate into countless reasons to feel and be happy. Choosing to steer ourselves toward that goodness and become part of it - as well as an advocate for it - is what brings us to a deep sense of completeness. This isn't about changing the world; it's about regularly making someone else's life a little easier, a little brighter, and a little better... perhaps even a stranger's life. When you wade into life's river of compassion, you make that river stronger. And as a result, the river makes you stronger. Which is to say, it feeds and enhances your sense of completeness. That's when you realize what is perhaps the most profound truth about being in an intimate relationship: You cannot seek out another to complete you. That will not work. But you can seek out another to share in your own completeness, and in turn, share in their completeness.

The Solution:

One of the most overlooked warning lights on the mind's dashboard of self-analysis is the, *"I can't live without 'X'"* indicator. Many people live their lives with several of these indicators flashing red, 24/7. The reason we tend to ignore them is because, when we have what we want, there isn't any urgency associated with these warning lights… until there is. After the unexpected implosion of a relationship, the passing of a loved one, or whatever calamity emerges from out of the blue, we suddenly find ourselves in crisis because we believe the lie that we can't live (or can't live happily) without whomever or whatever we've lost. It's only then that we understand what those flashing red lights were trying to tell us: In an unhealthy way, we've allowed our sense of self to become entangled with, and dependent upon, something or someone else.

So, how do we proactively keep this from happening? The solution is not that hard; it's the commitment to the solution that's tricky. To truly understand that no one else can complete us, we must set aside time to search within. We need to discover the inherent beauty we have within us, along with its unbridled potential to blossom. In short, we need to fall in love with ourselves. And this doesn't mean only seeing our best traits while overlooking our follies. It means falling in love with the work in progress that we are…

someone who's constantly learning and growing and who is loveable despite having more to learn and further to grow. You can't truly love yourself if you're only loving yourself in slices - you have to love the whole pie.

How is this accomplished? You can start with the widely known meditation method of staring into your own eyes in a mirror. Try it. While doing this, keep your mind as empty as you can - just stare and breathe. After a few minutes, you'll start to feel something akin to an inner smile from a rarely seen, innocent part of you that's just happy to be seen. Connecting with yourself in this way - again, with as little thought and commentary as possible - will inevitably expand the love and compassion you have for yourself. This simple method is only one example of a "going within" exercise that can remind you of how complete you are. It's a meditation that allows you to regularly see parts of yourself that you falsely believed were missing. And if you look within by engaging in this exercise (or something similar) for just a few minutes a day, you'll find that your need to be completed will fade, and an eagerness to share your completeness with others will expand.

LIE #13: I WON'T BE HAPPY UNTIL...

The Deception:

From microscopic bacteria to goldfish, dogs, and humans, we're all in a constant search for satisfaction and happiness. Achieving happiness is the fundamental drive that sponsors most people's actions (and inactions). But once we have our basic, physical needs met (which, sadly, too many of our fellow humans currently don't), achieving a state of happiness can become tangled up in what society convinces us happiness requires. And before we know it, we believe one of the most insidious lies of all: that happiness is conditional. This is also one of the sneakiest lies, because so many people unconsciously buy into it. Literally.

Media - and more specifically, marketing - contribute to this lie as we're fed a constant stream of images designed to convince us that we can't be truly happy until we acquire certain things or remake ourselves in certain ways. And that's when the insane race begins. We start chasing someone else's image of happiness without stopping to investigate whether that image is worth chasing. Compounding matters, those media images are always multiplying. They become a never-ending frenzy of changing requirements that keep happiness in the future. As soon as you catch and achieve one image, another image pops up, and the happiness goalpost moves downfield yet again... just out of reach.

The Truth:

There is no universal model for happiness. Happiness is subjective and different for everyone. One person's happy life circumstances could be another person's perpetual torture. Also, life is constantly changing. So, if you attempt to capture and freeze your happy life picture as a set of ideal circumstances, the forces of change will eventually find it and summarily unfreeze it. This fact of life illustrates the obvious: We must strive to live in an evolving state of happiness. All of us have done this before. We've all had the experience of losing interest in childhood toys as we've grown older. And we've observed that our ideal Saturday night has changed over the years as we've matured. This shows that happiness goes hand in hand with flexibility. Flexibility is what allows happiness to flourish and expand, often in ways we couldn't have predicted.

It may sound cliché, but nevertheless it's true that the best things in life are free. So, too, are the happiest things in life. If you want to experience deep, lasting happiness, don't go looking for it with a winning lottery ticket, in the halls of mansions, or on private jets. Seek it in fostered friendships, simple acts of help and kindness, unsolicited generosity, unexpected forgiveness, and true intimacy. These are the joys that resonate with our souls and are rooted in our highest nature. And because the potency of these joys comes from what you offer as a person, they require no condition from the outside world. This is true and timeless happiness.

The Solution:

As kids, most of us experienced the innocent joys of childhood… simple things that would make our day, keep us entertained for hours, and transport us to instant contentment. As adults, happiness and contentment seem much more complicated. But do they really have to be? The secret formula of childhood is that kids tend to live in the present moment. Adults, by comparison, tend to dwell on regrets from the past, fears for the future, and worrying about creating the perfect circumstances that fit their happiness model. But happiness will never be found in the past or in the future; it's a "right here, right now" phenomenon. And we'd all do well to live more in the present moment and be a bit more child-like in our daily lives. We adults should also learn to trust ourselves a little less and trust life a little more. When we cling to what we think we know about happiness, we leave little room to learn about its depths... to be guided to it by our intuition... to see how it's automatically delivered to us when we flow along with life's twists and turns instead of fighting them.

When we're working to beneficially change our world and change our lives, happiness can be a product of that effort even if we haven't yet reached our ideal. But if we're waiting for some set of conditions to be met before we can be happy, we'll be waiting for an eternity. Gratitude for what's good in our lives right now - as well as gratitude for the possibilities that lie ahead of us - is the key to unlocking happiness this instant.

LIE #14: I HAVE BAD LUCK

The Deception:

As a society, we use the word "luck" very causally in phrases such as, *"Good luck!"* and *"You're so lucky!"* and *"Wow, that was bad luck."* These sayings are used almost involuntarily by so many. But what is luck? Is it something we can give, possess, or be without? Is it a mysterious force of life that determines fate? Or is the word itself a thin veneer we use to conveniently name something we don't understand? Most definitions of luck include the word "chance." If you believe that chance or randomness is part of life, then it would follow that everyone has the same unpredictable, random luck. Sometimes it's good, sometimes it's bad, but in either case, it seems to be for no apparent reason. Following that logic further suggests that luck isn't something you have or don't have; it's something you experience. However, a higher analysis will lead you to a very important, self-reflective question: *"Why am I experiencing the luck that I'm experiencing?"* Many people dismiss any further investigation by declaring, *"There is no reason. It's just luck... that's the point."* But it's more interesting not to settle for that superficial answer and instead begin to contemplate a force of life that's much greater than mere chance. That force is you.

The Truth:

To get beneath the surface of what society calls "luck," we need to go beyond what could be called "the provable." Although this is more of an intuitive, spiritual endeavor, it's not devoid of reason and logic. In a way, we're investigating the source code of luck to see what creates it and what makes it tick. When we experience "good luck" or "bad luck," we're experiencing the result of an equation that we, often unconsciously, set into motion. Whether we directly perceive it or not, each of us is an independent part of a huge system that's evolving toward higher functionality. During this evolution, the individual parts of that system become not only self-aware but also aware of the greater system itself. It's not important what name we give this system. But as our awareness expands, it becomes clear that the system is always working in our favor - even and especially when we experience "bad luck."

Luck from the perspective of the mind or body is vastly different than luck from the perspective of the soul. Your body and mind together can misbehave like a child who throws a tantrum when things don't go the way they want. Your soul is like the wise parent who sees much, much further than the child can. It understands that what appears as bad luck is only part of an evolutionary growth process we all must go through. Your soul is the boundless part of you that draws into your life the experiences you need in order to evolve. Meanwhile, your mind and your body will no doubt label some of these experiences as bad luck. But if you earnestly look for it, deep down in your core of cores, you'll find the part of you that understands the reason for whatever difficulty you're experiencing - and is quietly at peace with it.

Of course, if we were all living with full awareness of and connection to our souls, we would look at our imperfect, personal world and see nothing but perfect evolution. And we'd see straight through the illusion of bad luck... seeing through the negative effects directly to their causes... seeing past the turmoil directly to its purpose... and seeing through the pain directly to its meaning. But we have bills to pay, children to feed, maladies to manage, and inequalities to solve. These life challenges require action, and we can't effectively engage them with our head in the clouds. Nevertheless, when we're tethered to this higher truth about luck, we become grounded during our challenges in a way that calms our inner storms and pulls us through those difficult times when we're down on our luck.

The Solution:

Growing beyond the "bad luck" mindset requires two things: self-responsibility and a willingness to change. For the idea of bad luck to survive, it requires a victim. Deny it that. Avoid inner monologues like, *"This shouldn't be happening to me"* or *"Someone else controls my destiny."* This isn't to suggest that injustice and inequality don't exist in our world - they certainly do. But inequalities aren't solved, luck doesn't change, and lives aren't improved by staying stuck in victimhood. That works against both self-responsibility and self-empowerment. As we've covered, it takes a spiritual perspective to effectively engage self-responsibility as it applies to "bad luck." Even if you don't know why your luck is currently so hard, taking the leap - or at least entertaining the possibility - that there's a good reason for it will give you greater inner peace and more courage. Once you begin to make that shift into a *"Life is happening for me, not to me"* mindset, then you're ready to ask yourself the two most important questions regarding bad luck: *"Why have I brought myself here?"* and *"What is life trying to get me to change?"*

Fostering this kind of inner humility is when you start directly interfacing with the behind-the-scenes, intrinsic intelligence of life itself. Think of this intelligence as a timeless universal awareness. Over millennia, countless cultures have labeled this awareness "God." Terminology and religion aside, if you're asking yourself those two questions, you'll be instantly plugged into the most effective self-improvement connection in the cosmos. Your intuition will then light up as you begin to understand new things about yourself, your circumstances, and why your luck shows up the way it does. Utilizing this tool of spiritual self-reflection, your life will dramatically change for one simple reason: You are willing to change. This isn't about becoming someone different; it's about improving your life navigation skills and how you interact with the world. Specifically, when taking responsibility for your luck, you'll begin to improve how you internalize your experiences, how you talk to yourself, how you treat your body, how you treat others, how you make and don't make assumptions, and what you believe about your own life's potential. Improving these things is what initiates a change in luck.

You may not be fully conscious of it, but your luck - whether it's good or bad - comes from you. And when you start positively adjusting how you think and how you live, your luck will vastly improve.

LIE #15: I'M A FOOL

The Deception:

Human newborns are among the most helpless creatures in the animal kingdom. For our first few years on this planet, we operate as adorably cute little fools. Entirely dependent on others during this time, we wouldn't last more than a few days without their help. By comparison, giraffes are on their hooves and walking around within a few hours of being born. Some species of birds can fly within a day of hatching. Sea turtles know exactly what to do and where to go as soon as they see the world for the first time. So, yes, compared to many of our fellow animals, we start out a bit behind the curve. And throughout each stage of our lives, we will no doubt act like fools from time to time. But there's nothing inherently foolish about us. This is true because, as humans, we have the capacity to observe the effects of our behavior and to then alter that behavior. It's clear, though, that many adult humans haven't yet matured enough to fully use that capacity. Still, whether utilized or not, this potential to learn and employ behavioral change exists within us all.

We most often call ourselves fools after we've made a mistake: *"I can't believe I did that... I knew better... now I've really messed things up... I'm such a fool!"* First, it's okay to be frustrated with ourselves, but that frustration is healthy only in the context of learning. And no one who is willing to learn from their mistakes can be a fool. Of course, we've all done things that made sense in the moment but, in retrospect, looked foolish. It's easy to see this while watching your own life's instant replays. However, you weren't a fool for making a bad choice; you just lacked a complete picture of what that choice would look like and feel like after you made it. We're all doing the best we can with our current understanding of ourselves and the world. And either consciously or unconsciously, we're collecting experiences that make us more aware and will eventually make our choices less foolish.

The Truth:

Sustaining the *"I'm a fool"* self-talk is often an unconscious expectation of perfection. Although, there are those among us who are self-compassionate by default. These easy-going people make mistakes and can shrug off most of them with a simple, *"I'll do better next time."* As long as they don't let this attitude devolve into apathy, that mindset is a blessing - both mentally and physically. Nothing can take you from healthy to high blood pressure faster than unrealistic expectations of yourself or of others.

It's vital to understand that making less foolish choices is a journey where progress is the name of the game, not perfection. This revelation can relieve a lot of pressure. And when you've relieved much of that pressure, you can more clearly see and be inspired by how far you've come. You can even look back at your "old self" and understand why you were that person. Consider that most people don't look at a beautifully preserved, classic sports car from the 1960s and say, *"What a technologically deficient, uncomfortable, backwardly designed, piece of polluting junk!"* Instead, we typically recognize a car like that as a "period piece," representing the best of what that era had to offer. In other words, those car designers were doing the best they knew how to do back then. Try to see your past blunders and the older versions of yourself the same way. Appreciate where you've been (even if it isn't pretty) while acknowledging that you're producing new models of yourself with new upgrades and improvements every day.

The Solution:

To understand the nuts and bolts of our temporary foolishness, we need to pop the hood on our internal processes. In life, when we play the fool, there's always a reason for it. In fact, there are infinite reasons, which differ from person to person. But like a good mechanic, we must investigate the malfunction and track down the problem. And our primary anti-fool fix-it tool is self-inquiry. *"What was the root of my foolish behavior? ... Was it innocent ignorance? ... Did I simply speak without thinking? ... Perhaps it was insensitivity - did I not consider someone else's perspective? ... Or maybe it was fear - did I lash out because I was afraid of a potential outcome?"* Wherever your investigation leads, it's important to be as objective as possible and constantly ground yourself in the truth that these missteps are not who you are. Who you are is the investigator who's hot on the trail of discovering your own higher nature and greater wisdom.

The second part of solving and understanding our foolishness requires that we contemplate a much larger truth: Foolishness has its place. In my previous book, *Glossary of Life – A Path to Joy, Balance, and Peace,* we took a deep dive into this concept. I'll summarize that deep dive here as it relates to the mistaken belief that your foolishness can ruin anyone or anything. To be blunt, you're simply not that powerful. If we all realized how powerfully our soul - often without the mind's permission - shapes and creates the circumstances of our lives, we'd be astounded. But if we realized how powerless we are to control or negatively impact the lives of others, we'd be even more astounded.

In the timeless reality of our soul - which is the only real and lasting reality we have - we're all instruments of evolution for one another. Though most are unaware of this, all are part of a mind-blowingly complex community of meticulously managed, intersecting life stories that would easily overwhelm all of humanity's most powerful supercomputers. Within this all-encompassing spiritual community, foolishness is never wasted. From our very limited human perspective, the outcome of foolishness can appear to us as unfortunate or tragic. But from a grander perspective, we can see that the sometimes difficult and painful result of foolish behavior is always for the long-term benefit of each soul affected by it.

To many, this concept may sound absurd and even callous. And it should never be used to justify negligence or a lack of self-responsibility. However, if we can speculate - only for a moment - that this bigger perspective is real, cracks begin to form in the crippling guilt felt by so many in the wake of their foolish behavior that they perceive has negatively impacted others.

It sounds preposterous, I know… this notion that absolutely nothing can happen to you - including traumatic injury or death - without your soul's authorization; and that everyone's life stories - along with their mistakes - are intricately intertwined with harmonic perfection. But it's a big Universe out there, and as the history of science has shown us, we're bound to discover that some of today's preposterous notions will become tomorrow's incontrovertible truths.

LIE #16: I'M LOST

The Deception:

When we feel lost, embedded in this feeling is usually the added feeling of being alone. But at any given
moment, tens of millions of souls on this planet are also
feeling lost. Therefore, it's not really possible to be lost
and alone when there're so many others who share this
experience with you. Think of people living today or

throughout human history who have inspired you. Want to guess one thing you have in common with all of them? At some point in their lives and along their journeys, they felt lost just like you have. And look around at your own friends and family. You're probably close enough with some of them to know firsthand that they've felt lost a few times in their lives. Even if you don't have that firsthand knowledge about them or anyone else, it's a safe assumption that everyone shares this experience. One reason we experience misery along with the feeling of being lost is that we've decided it's bad to be lost. When we feel lost, we often erroneously conclude that we must be defective or inferior in some way.

It isn't wrong to feel lost and alone on occasion. Anyone who has discovered anything - whether personally, professionally, or historically - has felt lost along the way to their discovery. Feeling lost is a temporary state. Recall the times you've felt lost, and then try to remember what it was that brought you out of those depths. Chances are, what saved the day for you was something new and unexpected - a change in circumstance, new information, help from an unexpected encounter, or a sudden insight. The reason that feeling lost always has an expiration date is because life is constantly changing. When you spot this pattern and understand its inevitability, feeling lost just becomes a waiting area - a temporary pause as your life shifts from one level to its next level.

The Truth:

Life is not designed as an impossible maze that we have no hope of navigating. There is always a way forward on our path, and there is always a solution to our problems. What can be confusing is that the solutions are often contrary to what we think they should be. Thinking, as it turns out, is like salting your food. Just the right amount of salt can magnificently enhance your meal. But too much salt can ruin the entire dish. When you're trying to find your way forward, intuition - with a sprinkle of thinking - is the best recipe.

Within each of us is a metaphorical compass. Much like an actual compass that detects and responds to Earth's magnetic field, your intuition detects a bigger picture that is far beyond what you can see. This inner, intuitive compass is always pointing to where you need to go and what you need to do to find your best outcome. But again, following your intuition is a *feeling* endeavor, not a thinking one. And observing its guidance - guidance that may seem illogical yet *feels* right - requires two things: 1) momentarily detaching yourself from concerns about the past; and 2) taking your focus off fears and rigid ideas about the future. When you do those two things, this doesn't activate your intuition; it shows you that your intuition has always been on. All you've ever had to do to hear it is be in the present moment.

Be prepared, though, because just like navigating the wilderness, sometimes the best way to your destination is to go around an obstacle, not over it or through it. And your newfound inner compass will sometimes take you in a direction that - in the short-term - seems to be leading away from where you want to be. But intuition is a long-range instrument. And when you can silence your thoughts enough to accurately read it, it becomes an instrument you can trust.

Aside from thinking too much about the past or the future, the thoughts that get us off course the quickest are those that doubt our own potential. If we falsely believe there's something wrong with the explorer (us), that distraction makes it very difficult to read our environment, trust ourselves, and trust our abilities. This can become a paralyzing, internal obstacle that leads directly to the feeling of being lost, alone, and on top of that, incompetent. But those self-deprecating thoughts are untrue. Anyone - and I do mean anyone - who remains teachable and open to being guided will find their way.

The Solution:

Our greatest ally in finding our way out of feeling lost is the virtue of patience. Having patience is much easier said than done. It can be excruciating to hang around waiting for life to change into a version you think you can manage. If you're waiting for that to happen, you'd better have a seat, because it's going to be a long, long wait. Despite life's unwillingness to follow your rules, even the most trying situations can be surprisingly manageable when you patiently engage them in increments. This methodical approach helps mitigate feelings of being overwhelmed and gives you a practical place to start.

The next time you don't know what to do about a problem or where to begin solving it, do something small that's right in front of you. This act could be as simple as getting yourself a cup of tea, splashing water on your face, bringing a little order to a messy workstation, or just taking a few deep breaths. So often, we can find our way forward when we momentarily divert ourselves from obsessing about finding our way forward. Small, incremental acts make us more productive by bringing us back to the present moment and out of the stressful future we've created in our minds.

Another benefit to grounding ourselves in the present moment is that, when our minds are quiet and focused, we can read the terrain and the language of life with less distraction. Life has a subtle (and sometimes not-so-subtle) language it uses to guide us and speak to us along our path. This language can be perceived in retrospect as we identify the many "red flags" we missed after making a poor choice. But taking note of these flags - whether ahead of us or behind us - is precisely how we learn life's language. With experience, we eventually establish an interface with life that's much like a pilot listening to an air traffic controller. The "tower" knows our speed and direction, where we're coming from, and where we'd like to go. When we tune in to the tower's unique messages meant solely for us, and when we muster the courage to trust those messages, we're safely and expeditiously guided toward our intended destination - or eventually to a destination that's even better than we had in mind. You may interpret this mysterious "tower" in any way you'd like. But suffice it to say, this benevolent guidance is, at its essence, simply what works. Obviously, there isn't one magic solution for each life lived; there are many different solutions of happiness for each individual. But when we fly with reckless abandon - disregarding the tower's instructions along with its warning messages and red flags - we miss the happy, invigorating experiences of life and instead fly right into painful, self-created difficulties.

One vital thing to remember when navigating your own feelings of being lost is to stay humble and open. Those two words are used more than once in this book because, when joined together, they can solve so much in life. In matters of feeling lost, there's a third word that integrates critically with humility and openness. That word is discernment. It's tempting to try to fix feeling lost by blindly following someone who claims they know the way. In this digital age, there's no shortage of viral cults of personality - especially in politics. But discernment - doing your own homework and searching your own soul - is a prerequisite for finding your way. Outsourcing that external and internal process to someone else is a recipe for brainwashing. No matter how long it takes or how many red flags you miss, and regardless of how many flights of questionable fancy you take, there is always a course correction that will lead you home. Wherever it is you roam, you can never be truly lost as long as you keep exploring.

LIE #17: I KNOW BEST

The Deception:

"I always knew precisely what to do and exactly how my life was going to turn out." ... said no self-honest person,

ever. If there's one thing we can count on, it's that life rarely - if ever - shows up precisely how we think it will. Over the span of decades, years, months, or even minutes, unexpected factors are woven into the fabric of life. Despite this, the wonderfully mixed blessing that is our human ego regularly tries to convince us otherwise. And so begins the deception and delusion that we know best. It's certainly understandable that our ego often adopts this perspective by default. Being comfortable with uncertainty is not a trait most of us were born with. Yet when we act from a place of well-meaning, know-it-all arrogance, it eventually compounds our troubles. And our self-aggrandizement usually doesn't end there. Once we've fooled ourselves into believing that we absolutely know what's best, we then see it as our mission to convince everyone else of the same. And if they don't listen to us or follow our advice, then our fear, anger, and anxiety can all become supercharged.

Most of us carry a collection of insecurities within us. Some are small, but others can be substantial. The one thing these insecurities have in common is a degree of self-disapproval and a longing for external validation. This internal dynamic can help feed negative emotions when we're scared because we secretly realize we don't know what's best - either for us or for our loved ones. And again, to protect itself, this prompts the ego to create a façade of being the one who always knows what to do or what to say.

The Truth:

Presently, each of us has but one seat in the theater of life… one view of the world's stage… and one experience filter through which to view it all. We think we see so much, and that's precisely why it's not easy to notice (much less admit) that our solitary perspective is very limited. It's not always possible for us to know the best tactic or outcome. There are often too many unseen variables. But if you try, you can no doubt think of times when circumstances looked undesirable, only to discover later that those same circumstances were an integral part of something better. Having the wisdom to reserve judgment in the face of what seems like disaster is a discipline that can be learned. It's hard work to learn that discipline, but it's far more difficult not to strive for it and instead be emotionally tossed around by the drama or uncertainty of the day. Making fearful and dark conclusions about life from our limited perspective drives us straight down the road to depression and anxiety. What's more, this negativity distorts our view of life in a way that makes us blind to positive, silver lining perspectives and out-of-the-box solutions.

Your mind wants you to believe that once you know the right decision or the right path, and it's all mapped out in front of you, then you can rest and have peace of mind. But that day will never come for the simple reason that you aren't supposed to be all-knowing. That's not how life is designed. You're in the movie of your life - both acting and directing - but the Universe is the producer, and it hates spoilers. Besides, life would be much less exhilarating if you could see all outcomes from the start and always knew best.

The Solution:

In many Eastern spiritual traditions, one of the most common doctrines taught is the concept of surrender. Modern cultures in the west tend to think negatively of surrender. Often confused with resignation (an act of giving up hope and succumbing to negativity), the deeper nature of surrender is usually misunderstood and associated with powerlessness and defeat. But from a spiritual perspective, surrendering to that which is beyond us is among the most courageous, potent, and effective things we can do. At its core, surrendering to the unknown acknowledges that we don't know best and are willing to be guided by higher wisdom. This is a decision not to strongarm life by forcing our way, and instead surf life's waves of circumstance - holding our agendas loosely so that we're nimble enough to intuitively change them.

The instructions for this fluid and skillful way of living can be summarized in one, all-important word. That word, once again, is humility. Without humility, we'll inevitably fall into the delusion that we can rely solely on our minds to guide us seamlessly through life. To be clear, the mind is not your enemy; it is a vital instrument you possess. But it's your whole experience of life - the street smarts of the soul, if you will - that should be at the helm, steering the ship. Living from that place means grounding yourself with the immortal advice of the Greek philosopher, Socrates.

He taught that we should, in a sense, make friends with not knowing. And he advocated that doing so gives us an ever-greater capacity to know more, and paradoxically, to become wiser by knowing that there's always more to know. That kind of humility also expands our capacity to laugh at ourselves and at life. Not taking either too seriously is in the highest tier of sage advice.

To further combat the lie that you know best, it's essential to have the intention of serving what's best for everyone within your scope of influence. If humility has an arch-enemy, it's self-centeredness. To nullify that tendency, always try to act on behalf of both your own and others' interests. You'll be notified very quickly if you start to become selfish or cocky. Like the Fire Chaser Beetle, which can detect a forest fire up to 80 miles away, the pervasive intelligence of life will instantly spot your smoldering selfishness. It will then automatically orchestrate negative experiences and encounters as warnings that you're not choosing optimally. And the more those warnings are ignored, the louder and more uncomfortable they will get. Life is pre-programmed to eventually turn arrogance into humiliation. But when you're on the lookout for life's warnings and constantly renewing your sense of humility, life will unfailingly support you.

Last, for those willing to experiment with a bit of Eastern spiritual practice, I'd like to introduce to you what is, in my opinion, one of the most powerful mantras ever written. The practice of chanting mantras dates back several millennia. Along with meditation, this rhythmic, verbal repetition can have the effect of grounding one in the present moment, calming the mind, and fortifying one's life intentions. Mantra repetition is a sort of tuning fork for the soul.

The Sanskrit mantra, *Soham Sarnam (SO-hah-m SAR-nah-m)*, is loosely translated as, *I AM THINE.* "Thine" refers to a greater awareness, which knows what we have yet to discover. As referenced earlier, you can think of this awareness as God, and/or you can think of it as an all-encompassing consciousness - a vast storehouse of knowledge that, since the beginning of time, has been both the keeper and the source of every artistic, spiritual, philosophical, and scientific truth discoverable. In short, this awareness is both the arena and the rulebook for the cosmos and has existed long before we ever came along. But this awareness is also integrated deep within our intuitive, higher self (or soul). When you repeat the mantra, *Soham Sarnam* (in Sanskrit or in any language), you're getting in touch with a higher part of yourself by acknowledging that your limited mind doesn't know best. This opens the door to being guided by that which does know best. That's why this mantra is so powerful, and it synchronizes perfectly with one of the most revered things the Buddha ever said: *"There is no enlightenment without extinguishing self-will."*

Now, before you tap out on Buddha's quote, remember that this whole enlightenment business is a very complex journey with deeper and deeper discoveries that unfold over time - a lot of time. But your personal journey of discovery both begins and continues with asking for help. And that's really what this mantra (or any mantra) is for - a friendly wave to a higher consciousness, along with the humble and often-repeated request, *"Take me higher."*

LIE #18: I KNOW WHO I AM

The Deception:

From ancient Egypt and Greece... from China's and India's days of antiquity... and from the earlier periods of many western cultures, humanity's most respected sages, philosophers, and leaders have expressed the benefits of discovering who you are. This common guidance through-out world history highlights that knowing yourself is the key to unlocking the totality of life. The purpose and meaning of it all... the happiness and fulfillment to be had... the anxiety and fear to be vanquished... the inner peace, inspiration, and love to be encountered... all of it depends on this singular expedition of looking deeply within.

"But hang on..." I can almost hear some of you say... *"I've read books, been on retreats, endured upheavals and trials, experienced breakthroughs of awareness and understanding... and I'm now at a stage where I know who I am. I know what does and doesn't make me happy, and I'm at peace with that. Why do I need to look any further?"* Those very words are familiar to me because I used to say them as well. And then life would surprise, unsettle, and transform me, and I'd say them again. And then more life would happen, causing me to reset myself anew, and I'd say those words to myself again and again and again.

The Truth:

Life eventually brings us to the realization that we can never cross the finish line and wave the checkered flag on knowing ourselves. The simple reason is that we're too big to comprehend all at once. Before we get into an existential discussion about the enormity of the human soul, take a quick look at your own life - this life. Notice how you've changed through the years and through each major stage of life. And then try to remember your happiest times during each of those life stages... when things just felt right, or at least felt okay. We can all look back at our younger selves and remark, *"Oh, what blissful ignorance I had!"* Of course, blissful ignorance has its place. Without it, the magic of childhood would be lost. But the point is that just when we feel content that we know who we are and how the world works, we discover new vistas of understanding that were once invisible to us.

This may seem like a clumsy stumble through the process of growing up, but it's perfect that we're not built to know ourselves, or life, all at once. Life is meant to be a heavenly meal at a 5-star restaurant with each course individually experienced in sequence. No one wants their soup, salad, entrée, and dessert all thrown together into a blender and served as a smoothie. The experience of time exists so we can savor each stage of growth and each level of awareness along the way. Only then can we look back at the entire meal of life - even at those servings that were unpleasant but necessary - and appreciate life's full, unique symphony of flavors.

Who you are amounts to so much more than who you know yourself to be. You are not a concoction of chromosomes and inherited traits - that's just the equipment you're currently using. You came to this life with many of your own qualities, fully independent of your parents and ancestors. And the depth of those qualities reaches far beyond your conscious awareness... until it doesn't. Most of us are immersed in our characters so deeply that we can only grasp a faint echo of who we are. As we grow and mature, that echo gets louder. And when we intentionally pursue the question, *"Who am I?"* we begin to track down the source of our echo. We begin to meet our soul. This pursuit, however, is a discovery of self, not an assembly of missing parts. Buried beneath the lies we believe about ourselves, and buried beneath our misperceptions of reality, is the full and complete essence of our true self - our enlightened self. That's what genuinely defines us and is hiding behind every person's ego.

The Solution:

Discovering who you are is less like a treasure hunt (looking for and suddenly finding a stash of gold) and more like a trail of breadcrumbs that, step-by-step, takes you down an adventurous road leading you home. This isn't about achieving or attaining anything; it's about realizing something spectacular about yourself that's been obscured by the distractions of this world. Once you embark on the road to knowing yourself, each day begins by scanning the code to your heart. Meaning that every emotion felt and every reaction observed become your guide. Good and bad feelings - and why you feel those feelings - are the signposts meant to keep you on the path to greater joy. Feelings of pleasure always require a source or a kindling. But feelings of true joy are object-less... they require nothing. They simply are. They have no "first cause" or prerequisite. Joy is what you're made of, and it's found by letting go of anything in your mind that isn't loving and isn't compassionate. That sounds easy, right? Of course, if it were easy, everyone would've already done it.

Knowing yourself is the Mount Everest of human endeavors, but let's take a step back and try to simplify this undertaking. The solution to the marvelous riddle of who you are is the same solution to every problem that humanity has ever faced: Love. Love is the master tool for any occasion, and without a doubt, it's the primary tool for self-discovery. If you look at yourself or look at the world around you without seeing love, then you've just identified a blind spot to knowing yourself. A word of advice, though: Considering the atrocities in our world, it's not recommended that you be too ambitious with this "love everyone" exercise at first (we'll talk more about extreme degrees of love and forgiveness later). It's better to start with smaller things, like trying to see the love behind the well-meaning words or actions of a friend who unintentionally offended you. Getting into the practice of shifting your perspective in this way - i.e., seeing the world from outside of yourself - is precisely what's necessary to truly know others. And you can't truly know yourself until you see a part of you in everyone else, and conversely, a part of them in you. Again, I know this is a tall order (or tall mountain, as it were), but there's no sidestepping it: If you want to discover your true nature and the true nature of reality, you must grow in love more than you ever thought possible.

This venture is the end game. It's why we're all here. It's the destination to which all roads lead. Yet, as we've discussed, our journey to this destination is a destination in itself. The countless detours and scenic routes of life are built into this process. We are innate explorers, and this world is here for our exploration. We temporarily attempt to find ourselves in things like possessions, careers, and relationships. Searching for one's identity in those ways is another rite of passage on the path to enlightenment. But as we become more aware, we'll understand that - while all those things are wonderful - they do not ultimately define us. The immutable truth of who we are lies in our heart of hearts and cannot be taken away by any chaos, tragedy, or calamity around us.

If you get nothing else from this book, take this one precept with you, and never stop contemplating it:

Seek first to Know Thyself, and all
that once appeared dark will become light.

PART TWO:

THE LIES
WE'VE BEEN TOLD

LIE #19: BEING GOOD IS BORING

The Deception:

On its surface, life seems like a setup. Many of its most pleasure-inducing stimulants are bad for us. Medical research is clear, for example, that indulging with abandon in salt, sugar, unhealthy fats, deep-fried foods, alcohol, and drugs severely heightens the risk of heart disease, stroke, cancer, and mental decline. *"Who cares?"* some say. *"Why should we die pristine? Why shouldn't we 'be bad' and indulge every great stimulant we can find for as long as we can, and then slide into the grave exclaiming, 'what a ride!'"* The problem with this strategy is that living an unhealthy life often results in a very unpleasant "slide into the grave," which can take much longer than we anticipated. And that's referring to the physical repercussions, to say nothing of that lifestyle's adverse mental health effects. "Being bad" for the sake of temporary pleasure or gain can also take the form of cheating in a monogamous relationship, cheating on your taxes, or stealing someone else's property. Though temporarily easy, profitable, or fun, "being bad" in those ways (among others) runs up a debt that eventually must be paid with an enormous amount of interest (both literally and figuratively).

But why? Why is life set up this way? Why is the sweetest nectar of life, along with things that would seem to make life easier, laced with long-term poison? These are humanity's desperate, universal questions about impulsive pleasures. To answer these questions, it's necessary to pose a few related ones, such as: Are these decadent things really the sweetest nectar life has to offer? Can something be truly fulfilling if it isn't beneficial for you and for all involved? Are we being tormented for the sake of entertainment by some deranged deity? Or, are we being given an encoded opportunity and a secret invitation to seek out higher experiences?

The Truth:

As defined here, "being bad" is making choices that don't serve our long-term benefit. Choices that do serve our long-term benefit are usually paid for with short-term cost. This is true on a personal level just as it's true on a cultural, environmental, or planetary level. But we live in a developing society that hasn't fully embraced this sustainable life formula. Much of the developed world (and quite a few of its leaders) are still like five-year-old children who want what they want, and they want it NOW. As a result, wasteful and extravagant comfort is hoarded by a minority, many of whom refuse to share their abundance with countless millions who live without basic needs.

But let's bring this back down to a personal level. "Being good" and making choices that serve you is not about being perfect; it's about being conscious. When you make a habit of watching yourself and noticing the motivation behind your choices, those choices tend to get better. Sure, you may not choose the highest choice every time, but you'll develop an advance awareness of what certain choices cost. This means you'll more often catch your ego (a.k.a., the devil on your shoulder) poorly justifying a costly choice that you'll regret later. Understanding this internal process helps free you from being enslaved by your desires. That's when a breakthrough happens, and your entire tempo of life becomes elevated. You'll then find that choosing higher makes you feel good in much deeper ways than fleeting, short-term pleasures could ever touch. That's because - in those moments - you aren't just making a good choice; you're choosing to be the version of yourself that, deep down, you respect most. And there is no drug, drink, or junk food that can match that rush of healthy pride in yourself. Additionally, this isn't a buzz that fades after a few hours; it sinks into your very being. You will noticeably feel your capabilities, as well as the potential for your life, incrementally expand after each choice you make of which you are proud.

The Solution:

A practical place to start "being good" is to choose the lesser of two evils. It's perfectly prudent to ease into making better choices by continuing to make bad ones - but less bad. Try this: If you're currently starting each morning with a greasy sausage and double cheese biscuit accompanied by a supertanker-size dessert coffee, perhaps instead choose to swap out the sausage for a slice of ham and swap the large dessert coffee for a small one. Then, after a while, you might try a lightly buttered egg bagel (with a single slice of cheese), along with a moderately sweetened, regular coffee. And who knows... maybe one day a week you'll get a little crazy and have a bowl of blueberry and banana oatmeal with an orange juice. Throughout this process, pay close attention to how these choices make you feel - both physically and psychologically. You may find that making better choices evolves into an exciting, virtual sporting event. You become a running back, trying not to get tackled by a double bacon cheeseburger at lunchtime… or a race car driver expertly swerving to avoid the "HOT DO-NUTS NOW" drive-thru at 11:00PM. Your victories will have a next-level sweetness to them, and your defeats - provided you refrain from harsh self-judgment - will sting a bit, but they'll be beneficially instructive. As your choices improve, the lower, destructive pleasures in your life are traded for "classic" pleasures… pleasures (including from food) that are very enjoyable but have fewer strings attached.

As with most facets of life, something that's beneficial in a measured dose can work against you in mass quantity. This also holds true for self-discipline. We're all different, and we all have varying comfort zones that fit who we are and the life we've crafted. Finding your unique formula for what's not too tight and not too loose is something that requires experimentation (and occasionally, input from a cardiologist). But if your enduring intention is to live an enjoyable and sustainable life, then you will inevitably find your balance and find your way to being… mostly good.

LIE #20: YOU CAN'T CHANGE THE WORLD

The Deception:

Critics have a relatively easy job. Their self-appointed task is to poke holes in things - to shine a sometimes negative light on the grand plans, ideas, or endeavors of others. Any chaser of dreams who cannot endure an inevitable barrage of critics might need to reevaluate their dreams or their willingness to pursue them. Dreaming a new idea and deciding to put it out into the world can lead to a metaphorical blast furnace of opposition and skepticism. However, blast furnaces exist for a reason, and purifying precious metals is one of them. Step number one for making one's dream a reality is to willingly lean into the purifying furnace of critics. In fact, this may be the most important step because being open to constructive criticism can make your dreams even better.

Outside the bounds of constructive criticism, there will be professional cynics (including the cynic in your own mind) suggesting that not only can you not change the world, but you can't even change *your* world. As we can see, the world changes constantly, and people change their own personal worlds all the time. Look around at pretty much anything: lightbulbs, phones, airplanes, the World Food Bank, yoga studios - few things exist in this world that weren't driven into existence by an idea for change. The same mechanism exists in your own life. Of course, things happen, and the unexpected can radically shift your circumstances. But you're the one who decides what those circumstances mean and how you will or will not change in the face of them. Although, change can be somewhat relative. Holding your ground and maintaining your stance (or who you are) in the face of a cynical environment can require refortifying your existing ideals in new ways. This is like a ship, regularly battered at sea, whose every plank must eventually be repaired or replaced for the vessel to remain seaworthy and to remain the same ship. But after enough refortifying, is it the same ship? In ancient Greece, this philosophical riddle was known as the Ship of Theseus, and it illustrates how we change throughout our lives while, in many ways, staying the same.

The Truth:

Getting back to the general idea behind this lie, it's necessary to concede that there is an element of truth in the phrase, *"You can't change the world."* That is, as long as we add, *"by yourself"* to that phrase. In the long, destructive history of wildfires, there's no shortage of blazes that were started by a single match or a single spark. And while these tiny sources of heat were responsible for thousands of scorched acres, it's often dry kindling and swift winds that carry the ensuing flames of change across the landscape. Meaningful change in the world - or within an individual life - also requires metaphorical kindling and wind in the form of support. But regardless of how much support or help you have from others, that assistance cannot be utilized without the spark of an idea, the intention to change something, and above all, the belief that you can.

The French poet and novelist, Victor Hugo, famously wrote, *"Nothing... is so powerful as an idea whose time has come."* When you encounter the intersection of an idea and the right time for that idea to take hold, nothing can stop you. Whether it's time to stop smoking, take up a new hobby, change your career, or create something to share with the world, if you're earnestly willing to take whatever leap lies before you, you'll be caught and carried, and the world - your world - will be better for it.

The Solution:

So, once you've decided you want to change the world, where do you start? The answer: Look down at your feet, because wherever your feet are, that's where change begins. I mean this literally. If you're walking down a street, perhaps you've just stepped over a piece of trash you can pick up and put in a nearby garbage can. If you're at home, think of something unexpectedly nice you can do for a housemate or a neighbor. If you're at work, look for an opportunity to help a co-worker in a way they never expected. And if you have a friend or family member who has a special event coming up, make an extra effort to show up and support them. Or maybe you've read an inspiring story in your local news about someone who made a difference. Consider taking a few moments to send a quick, complimentary note to them.

The point is, anything positive you do in your own environment changes both the people and the world around you. Through encouragement and example, you become "patient zero" of a wonderful pandemic. Reaching out in support of someone energizes them to support others, and that virus of uplifting support and change continues to spread. This ripple effect starts with doing small things that are right in front of you. That's how you change the world. And remember, nothing impedes this process more than thinking that you must do something big to make a difference. In this world, the simplest and most effective formula for happiness is to be of help to others. When we engage that basic mission of being a good human, we're giving to life what we'd like to receive from life. And in reality's grand, energetic exchange, what we put into the world, we get back several fold.

Beyond the physical aspects of helping each other, there are metaphysical avenues of helping that are no less significant. In the wake of tragedy or crisis, we've all heard the phrase, *"Sending thoughts and prayers."* Although usually well-intentioned, this phrase sometimes becomes a substitute for action (particularly in politics). However, the world that we seek to change is more complex than our five senses can grasp. As quantum physicists have discovered, the entirety of our physical world is connected in ways that we can observe but don't yet fully understand. What science does understand is that every single one of us is integrated into the same, all-encompassing, quantum field of energy. To put this in simpler terms, we're all individual waves that appear separate but are fundamentally part of the same ocean. And that's not just a pretty metaphor; it's a scientific principle of physics that's been experimentally observed and mathematically proven. Everything and everyone exist as a massive soup of subatomic particles that are all behaving in different ways. Throughout the known Universe, no part of that soup is disconnected from any other part.

So, don't underestimate the power of your thoughts, prayers, feelings, or intentions about anyone, no matter how physically far away they are. When you open yourself to this scientific reality, you'll be amazed to discover how connected we all are and how healing and supportive it can be to hold someone in your heart. This is the subtle science of human spiritual connection, and it can go a long way to truly changing our world.

LIE #21: YOU CAN'T ESCAPE YOUR PAST

The Deception:

Many people were either raised with or later adopted the mistaken mindset that their reputation is who they are. This is another way of saying that their past defines them. Whenever you become aware of someone's reputation, the only thing you've become aware of is that person's past. It's only a part of their story, which, unless you're interacting with them in real-time, is old news. So often, we believe we know someone based on their reputation, but that assumption ignores what we already know about life: It can change in an instant, and so can we. Maturing is not a linear, predictable process. Seismic shifts in awareness and behavior can occur because of traumatic upheavals, inspiring interactions with others, or sudden breakthroughs in understanding that arise for no apparent reason. You don't know what has happened in a person's life - or how they've changed - since you became aware of their reputation, or even last interacted with them. This isn't to say you should ignore information about someone's past, nor should you discount your prior experiences with them. But evaluating whatever information you have about them in a less rigid way will keep you from fixating on their past while trying to interact with them in the present. This practice will also protect you from getting caught in your past when regretfully remembering your own missteps.

We can't sidestep the fact that past actions can have consequences that reverberate through a lifetime. Yet while some of those consequences are inescapable (like a life prison sentence), we can always escape our past by becoming someone different in the present. When we change, whether we're incarcerated or not, our past no longer has sway over who we are.

The Truth:

Though who we choose to be is not controlled by our past, our past is indelibly part of our story. In that respect, the past is forever within us. But it doesn't have to be operative within us. It's purely an archive - a museum, of sorts. And like all museums, it tells a story of what's been - not a story of what is or what will be. It's prudent to use the museum of our past as a resource to guide us as we make moment to moment decisions. Every uncomfortable result and cringe-worthy replay of yesterday become beacons on our personal path to being better and doing better. Our past illustrates that we can't always get it right, but our main job is simply to try. The intention to be better and do better has tremendous power over how our lives unfold. You've probably heard the saying, *"Good intentions pave the way to hell."* This is fundamentally false. Without a doubt, good intentions can occasionally backfire, and we may accidentally create the opposite of what we want. But the "good" part of the intention is still there. And if you don't give up on that, it's much easier to dust yourself off, learn the lesson, change the strategy, and move forward with that same good intention. It's this enduring mindset - coupled with equal parts humility and unselfishness - that redirects the "hell" of unintended results into nothing more than a brief detour.

The Solution:

There are two thought exercises that can assist in moving beyond your past. Both can be used daily or as often as you'd like. Let's call the first one the "clean slate" exercise. It consists of asking yourself a series of questions: *"If no one knew anything about me, and I could start from scratch, what would I change? How would I behave? How would I speak to people? What kind of person would I choose to be?"* These questions aren't meant to suggest you should try to be something you're not; their potential benefit is for you to envision the highest version of yourself that you can imagine, and then reverse engineer the process of becoming that person... even attempting to feel what it would feel like to be that person. This "clean slate" exercise will quickly reveal that this kind of aspiration leads to a happier life. That's not to say you must be your best self unfailingly; but pointing yourself in that general direction will inevitably bring more light and more love into your life.

The second thought exercise is more of a behavioral diagnostic and is somewhat less subtle. Early in life, as I was trying to figure myself out, I was fortunate to explore two different career paths: one as a police officer, the other as a middle school science teacher. Curiously, I heard the same warning in police academy as I did in teacher training: *"Don't do or say anything in the field (or in the classroom) that you wouldn't want to see on the evening news."* Both training programs correctly emphasized that those entrusted with our safety and those entrusted with our children are exposed to intense public scrutiny. As explained earlier, your reputation is not who you are. But being cast as someone you don't want to be is, for many, a solid incentive for good behavior. That's why this "evening news" exercise can be so effective. The danger of falling too deeply into this exercise, of course, is finding yourself psychologically handcuffed to your reputation, especially if you were to be - very publicly - wrongfully accused of something. In that scenario, knowing the truth, remembering who you are, and holding to your integrity, you might not care too much what the world misbelieves about you.

For most, being tied to one's image is a profound mental health liability should that image ever be tarnished. To limit this liability, it's vital to remember that you and everyone around you are sculptures of life, and those sculptures are never complete. You don't need to be embarrassed about whatever it is you've done, said, not done, or not said. The only thing you need to do is keep sculpting yourself and never stop. No difficult experience is ever wasted if you turn that experience into your clay, constantly spinning the potter's wheel of your life as you continually sculpt over the past by living fully in the present.

LIE #22: YOU ARE YOUR ACCOMPLISHMENTS

The Deception:

A significant source of insecurity and anxiety in our modern world is the burning drive to accomplish. This drive isn't a bad thing, as it fuels progress in virtually every human endeavor. But while the drive to achieve is, for the most part, beneficial to society, it can be detrimental on a personal level if left unchecked. This lingering liability centers around the lie that who we are is defined by our accomplishments or by our chosen work. Like many philosophical positions, this one comes with a small qualifier: Among the countless career paths available, if one were to choose a job that dishonorably inflicts harm on others (a lieutenant in the Mafia, for example), then one has not chosen a career but rather a dark persona, void of legitimate accomplishment or benefit to society. That said, what you do for a living or what you've accomplished is not an inherent character trait. The kind of person you choose to be while doing what you do is what reflects who you are... or at least who you are at a given stage in life.

If you become too self-identified with accomplishing a particular task at your job, as a parent, or even with a hobby, you'll begin to feel an uneasiness slithering its way into your daily efforts, and that will make those efforts less enjoyable. This isn't a rebuke for exercising discipline or setting goals; it's an invitation to recognize that who you are is much bigger and more profound than your goals. No one in your life has a relationship with your goals. Your loved ones

can't confide in them or call them for advice or encouragement. And when those close to you are in crisis, your goals
cannot offer a shoulder to cry on. That stuff - the important
stuff in life - is all you, not anything you've accomplished.

The Truth:

If you feel like you don't matter, and you need a pat
on the back or a feather in your cap, try this on: You are
and always have been the only thing you've ever needed to
be - a soul who has come to this time and place to learn and
grow in the best way you know how. And whether you're
aware of it or not, you are incredibly courageous - and yes,
accomplished - for just showing up in this life. Of all the
expressions of consciousness in this world, for whatever
reason and by whatever mechanism, you earned a ticket
as a human being. And that's an extraordinary opportunity.
So, even if you don't think you've got it together, you made
it this far. Now, where do you go from here?

Knowing that you're already accomplished, worthy -
and dare I say, great - you don't need to achieve anything
else to maintain that. This leaves you with one extraordinary mission in life: to imagine, create, and explore new
ways to experience your inherent greatness. And that can
be accomplished in innumerable ways - from something
as small as growing a charming, windowsill garden to
something as big as solving nuclear fusion... and anything
in between. Every human endeavor has equal merit in the
context of making the world a little brighter, a little easier,
or a little kinder. It's virtually impossible to waste your life if

you make a habit of trying to be the best person you know how to be. And if you fail at that, the experience will still be fuel for growth and of benefit to your soul.

The truth is that you're on a never-ending journey of accomplishment through learning. This didn't start when you were born, and it doesn't end when you die. We'll talk more about that in a later chapter, but for now, know that fulfillment in life can be found in the core of who you are. And the faster you stop searching for that fulfillment exclusively from external accomplishments, the faster you'll experience it, and paradoxically, the easier external accomplishment will become.

The Solution:

There're only so many ways the same thing can be said differently, but here again, we're back to the importance of living in the now (a.k.a. mindfulness). To uncouple from the habit of identifying with accomplishment while simultaneously engaging the thrill of pursuing it, you must focus on your endeavors one frame at a time. Obsessing with a goal that's too far in the future will stress you out and distract from your immediate efforts. A useful tip: Concentrate on having good form in whatever you're doing right now... turning a screwdriver, painting a wall, building a spreadsheet, counseling a co-worker... anything. Try to detect if there's even the slightest room for improvement in your focus. Professional athletes often describe a "flow state" in which they enter a mental and physical zone where they become totally immersed in their game, so much so that they hardly need to think about their actions. Even though they're not necessarily focused on a particular result while immersed in that state, accomplishing their desired result becomes almost effortless. This process is flowing toward accomplishment rather than grinding toward it and greatly reduces thought-based stress. And remember, it all starts with focusing on one frame of an endeavor and one frame of life at a time.

Much too often, people of a certain age believe the lie that their days of accomplishment have passed. They mistakenly compound that lie with another: They believe they aren't who they once were because they can no longer do what they once did. Fortunately, the human soul is timeless; it doesn't care how old its current body is. And while it's true that certain pursuits are no longer prudent at later stages in life, once we connect to the truth of who we are, we'll see that an entirely new world of accomplishment is set before us... a world of ever new joy, contentment, wisdom, and connection. As we age, the illusion is that we're on a downward trajectory. But for those who refuse to define themselves by worldly measures, breathtaking and elevated life experiences will be discovered just over the horizon. And when the sun sets on our time here, the question that will matter most isn't, *"What did I do with my life?"* ... it will be... *"Who did I become with my life?"*

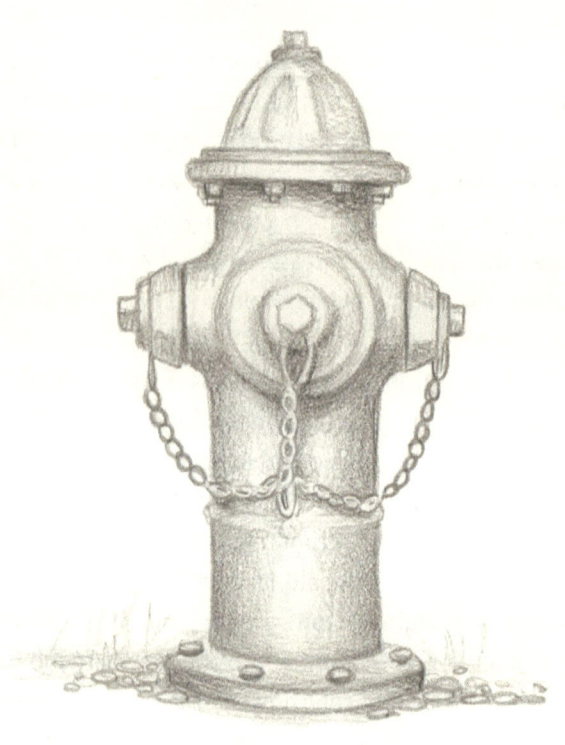

LIE #23: YOU MUST FIGHT FIRE WITH FIRE

The Deception:

Of all the lies covered in this book, the analysis of this one is perhaps the most nuanced. That's because the discussion of this lie begins by contradicting it. If we were to tell a law enforcement officer or a soldier that they don't have to fight fire with fire, they'd laugh in our face - and rightly so. The heroic souls who choose those selfless careers keep lawlessness at bay and literally hold the fabric of society together. Before we even begin a surgical deconstruction of this lie, full recognition of the reality in which these individuals live is necessary. At present, there are more than a few bad actors in our world who are very confused about the intrinsic value of human life. Sometimes, when confronted with these lost, aggressive souls, there's no option that seems viable other than fighting fire with fire, especially in the face of injustice, oppression, or cruelty. We live in an adolescent society that has a long way to grow before it can be called healthy. A global society, though, is composed of individuals who are each on their own evolutionary journey. Frequently, those journeys significantly outpace the evolution of society at large. It is within that context that we'll engage this lie.

Conventional thinking would suggest that if you aren't willing to fight fire with fire, then you live in a pacifist fantasy land. However, there is an entire division of the armed forces, numbering thousands of service personnel, who don't fight fire with fire. In fact, they're required not to. These brave souls in uniform are often deployed to war zones but carry no weapons. They are called the Chaplain Corps and are considered an exceptionally valuable asset of militaries around the world. Military chaplains dedicate their lives to supporting the mental, spiritual, and emotional well-being of those who serve in unthinkable conditions. Chaplains do not fight with the fires of war; instead, they arm soldiers with faith and fortitude so those soldiers can fight their own invisible yet destructive psychological fires within.

To further dispel the belief that we all must fight fire with fire, we turn to examples from world history. Look no further than the colossal influencers of old - including famous religious avatars, enlightened politicians, and civil rights leaders. Many of the most well-known rejected violence and advocated for peaceful resolution of conflict. This approach immensely amplified the impact of their message and showcased how they inspired and changed the world.

The Truth:

"If you wait by the river long enough, you will see the body of your enemy float by." This is a well-known, ancient Chinese proverb, written to convey two points: 1) Violence isn't sustainable because it always breeds more violence; and 2) Violence is a bloodthirsty beast that is kept alive by feeding on those who use it. Both of these points are true not only about physical violence but psychological and emotional violence as well. Still, we're faced with daily atrocities, which create an imbalance that attracts violence in return. As a result, we find ourselves trapped on a perpetual violence pendulum.

How then do we free ourselves? The answer is that we can't unless we unlearn what many of us were taught about the existence of evil. Evil does not exist as a force of its own. What we call evil is extreme confusion coupled with a lack of compassion. There are despots, terrorists, and serial killers who have fallen deeply into that abyss, but no one - and I mean no one - has a soul that is inherently evil or beyond redemption. As hard as this may be to fathom, once we consider this possibility, it resets the scope through which we view our enemies. It makes us pause before attempting to wipe them out without a second thought. To be sure, we still have to deal with them, but in doing so, we'll see them as confused parts of ourselves and our society that require healing. And healing can't happen unless the source of the infection is addressed, not just the symptom. This is the per-spective that's needed, for example, to fund the expansion of mental healthcare for extremely troubled and potentially violent individuals; or build an international coalition to fight the abject poverty that fuels terrorist recruitment.

Wisdom and common sense dictate that we fight fire with fire suppressant, not with fire itself. Obviously, it's im-practical to expect this to happen overnight. But in time, as more individuals and nations begin to invest less in weap-ons and more in solutions, humankind's cycle of violence will move closer to ending.

The Solution:

Let's take a break from all this grandiose talk of how to achieve world peace. After all, world peace begins with peace in the hearts and minds of individuals. As individuals, it's easy to be swept into torrents of political, religious, or cultural intolerance, especially if our friends and family are caught in them. And this dynamic isn't limited to large-scale geopolitics. Intolerant ideologies can happen with bullies on a playground... or in local churches or clubs that adopt bigoted policies... or in a company enacting exclusionary business practices. If we say or do nothing in response to these things, we become complicit. But what tactics can we use to navigate these torrents and push back on them without fighting with fiery aggression? One answer is found in the earlier reference to military chaplains. Again, chaplains are not adversarial. Their job is to offer the guiding light of a higher perspective. They aren't fighting in personal opposition to anyone; they exist for the benefit of everyone. And like doctors administering care while adhering to the Hippocratic Oath regardless of their patient's deservingness, chaplains would minister to soldiers on either side of a conflict, given the opportunity. So, one approach to becoming your own brand of activist in difficult scenarios is to ask yourself, *"How can I be more chaplain-like in my effort to influence hearts and minds?"*

No template can address this question for every situation. However, there are a few basic guidelines that can help you engage without fighting with fire. First, try to keep judgment out of the picture. You may be dealing with confused souls, but if you're looking down on them, they'll feel this a mile away. Second, keep your own ego in check by showing a willingness to listen and perhaps learn something you didn't expect to learn. And third, be prepared to walk away if necessary - as amicably as possible - while never letting go of your peaceful intentions. Getting angry and making enemies slams the door on the potential for future dialog. People can certainly change, but in the meantime, parting ways with an organization or group that no longer resonates with you might be prudent... at least for a time. Your amicable demeanor - without the distraction of insults or drama - may well cause other members of the group to self-reflect and change in ways you might not expect.

Most of the utopian fantasy stories that've ever been written have one commonality: People within those stories usually work out their differences without resorting to violence. From a macro perspective, the violence of fighting fire with fire is a messy but necessary stage of evolution through which individuals, nations, and cultures must pass. Despite that, it serves us all to continue striving - in some cases, inch by inch - for the nonviolent utopia of our dreams. But I'll conclude this chapter as I began it - with immense gratitude and admiration for those in uniform who keep our current world from descending into chaos and anarchy. They are the guardians of humanity's growth process, and they're the ones who afford us all the space and time to pursue our limitless journey of spiritual evolution.

LIE #24: SOME THINGS ARE UNFORGIVABLE

The Deception:

We need to carefully ease into deconstructing this lie, as the subject of forgiveness can be a trigger for many. For those who have experienced significant suffering and trauma at the hands of others, this chapter might be a steep climb. But if there's anyone in your life for whom you're harboring intense animosity, this will be a worthwhile climb.

From the global arena of war, oppression, and genocide to the interpersonal landscape of bullying, abusive relationships, and even murder, life among fellow humans can be so grueling that, at times, it feels as if we've been catapulted beyond the reach of forgiveness. In the wake of something especially injurious, our limits will undoubtedly be reached. However, if there's one defining trait of our species, it's our insatiable drive to find our limits and exceed them. The pursuit of ever-higher compassion is no exception, and compassion is the primary sponsor of seemingly superhuman forgiveness. First, though, we need to make one thing crystal clear: Forgiving someone is not synonymous with excusing their behavior or pardoning them from consequences. That said, forgiveness allows us to let go of toxic negativity regardless of whether contact is even made with the offender or if the offender is ever held accountable. But we need to hit the brakes right here, because in the immediate aftermath of a seemingly unforgivable act, most people feel intense bitterness and resentment. And that's okay. Forgiveness is a process that must unfold in its own time, and that process varies from person to person. As you grow in compassion, will forgiving someone who hurt you take less time? Of course it will. In the meantime, it's vital to observe your feelings and recognize where you are on your journey of forgiveness without judging yourself for being there.

The Truth:

Forgiveness research is currently in its infancy, but there have been several well-credentialed clinical studies that suggest forgiveness measurably decreases anxiety, depression, and stress. These studies further indicate that forgiveness can lead to better sleep and lower blood pressure. For anyone who's experienced the tense vitriol that comes with thinking or speaking about someone they refuse to forgive, the results of these studies should come as no surprise. There's nothing physically or psychologically pleasant about being in a state of unforgiveness. Yet, according to medical science, withholding forgiveness can negatively impact our health. And the truth is, there's only one prescription for healing that condition. (If only forgiveness could come in a pill.)

One alluring aspect of withholding forgiveness is a temporary rush of power. When we refuse to forgive, there's nothing anyone can do about it. However, the real dynamic at play is that - in addition to what they've done that hurt us - they are now controlling our state of mind via our involuntary response of anger. "Involuntary" is the key word here. It implies a lack of control. And again, our lack of a controlled response to the offending party is harming us, not them.

There's an additional psychological liability that comes with holding back forgiveness. When you refuse to forgive someone, you are choosing to live in the past. And when you make a habit of living in the past with those around you, your internal relationship - that is, your relationship with yourself - usually follows suit. If you have a hard time forgiving others, it's very likely you'll also have a hard time forgiving yourself. To break this pattern, you must start somewhere, and the best place to start is inside. Whatever you've done that you're struggling to forgive yourself for, try to view it in the context of your entire life. Maybe it was a momentary lapse in judgment. Or perhaps you incrementally fell into a cycle of bad choices until things got out of control. But do these very human mistakes really define the totality of who you are? Do they represent every second of your days? Do they erase or taint your childhood and anything good you've ever done since then? Do they stop you from changing or growing into a better person? Allow me to save you the time of contemplating those four questions, because the answers to them are no, no, no and no. To err is human, and if your intention is to err less often, then forgiving yourself for being human will make that process much easier.

The Solution:

Whether we see ourselves as victims or perpetrators, one thing that makes us despondent in the wake of difficult circumstances is our mistaken belief that there's no way to fix what's been broken. We then conclude that life is all depressingly downhill from there. While it's true that actions have consequences and lives change as a result of them, life can heal around those consequences and become something beautiful despite them. To expound on that concept, a discussion of the larger trajectory of life and the soul is needed... but we'll save that for the last chapter. For now, let's focus on immediate solutions that enable forgiveness.

As is often the case, solutions are found by attempting to follow the examples of others who've already implemented them - and who've done so in extraordinary ways. We're talking here about a mother who found it in her heart to forgive her son's murderer, then successfully pleaded with a court to stay the man's execution. And a daughter, severely abused through childhood by her mother, who after decades of estrangement, found the compassion to care for her mother during her final weeks of life. And a husband, whose pregnant wife and child were killed in a car accident, who chose to forgive and even befriend the grief-stricken driver at fault. Each one of these individuals from those true stories had remarkably similar accounts of their path to forgiveness. The more they fed the forces of rage and blame within them, the more difficult it became to reconcile their loss. But when they separated the perpetrator from the incident - along with the many difficult factors that led to it - they were finally able to let go of their dark feelings. As soon as they did, an unexpected lightness and peace replaced those dark feelings.

The reason that healing between forgiver and offender succeeds is because, as mentioned before, life is essentially a constant exchange of energy. What you send out into life inevitably comes back to you. And so it follows that whatever you give to others, you are essentially giving to yourself. Imagine the incredible relief and indescribable emotion felt by each of the people who were forgiven in those three stories. That was likely a gift they never expected - even in their wildest dreams. It was equivalent to dropping an atomic forgiveness bomb whose blast radius eliminated a vast expanse of anguish and suffering felt by both offender and forgiver. Deep within every human heart there exists such a nuclear arsenal of compassion and forgiveness... as well as the capability to use it.

LIE #25: THERE ISN'T ENOUGH

The Deception:

Tackling this lie requires a practical definition of the word "enough." In the context of saying, *"I don't have enough,"* it's a useful exercise to do a quick image search for the term, "abject poverty." Once you see those photos (and realize that well over half a billion people currently live in those conditions), you're ready to have a grounded conversation about what "enough" is. This exercise isn't meant to shame you. In our familiar First World living conditions, it's easy to lose perspective on what true scarcity looks like. But when negotiating the stressful rapids of modern life while striving for balanced mental health, it's critical to remind ourselves of how much we take for granted.

Gandhi famously said, *"The world has enough for everyone's need but not enough for everyone's greed."* Even today, with over 8 billion people on this planet, his words still ring true. It's estimated that between commercial and residential inefficiencies, more than one-third of all food produced for human consumption is wasted. If even a fraction of that waste were recovered, it would be enough to all but end global food scarcity. We are a species that has been to the moon and back. The problem with feeding the hungry is well within our capacity to solve. But collectively, we need to care more about it to solve it. Gandhi also encouraged us to be the change we wish to see in the world and not wait for others to change before doing so ourselves. With regard to feeding the hungry, "being the change" can be as simple as eating your leftover food and, if you're able, making regular contributions to your local food bank.

Let's switch gears to another aspect of scarcity: time. Most of us have used the phrase, *"There aren't enough hours in the day!"* Here again, we may be a bit out of touch with stark reality. Consider the single mother who must work two jobs to feed her kids and keep a roof over their heads, while somehow finding enough time to accomplish essential household tasks. The word "essential" is where many of us stumble. When we're blessed with abundant leisure time, the activities we tend to classify as essential can grow in number and lessen in importance. But like the abject poverty exercise above, it serves us - in those exasperating, time-crunch moments - to acknowledge how much less time we'd have if we worked a second or third job to support a family. Still, we are natural prioritizers. And although our ability to prudently prioritize is often a work in progress, what's most important will make its way to the forefront. Many of us, for example, always find time to brush our teeth at night. And though we never plan for it, if we need to recover from an illness or visit a loved one in the hospital, we make time for those things because we recognize they're important.

The Truth:

The term "rat race" is informally defined as the exhaustingly competitive, self-defeating pursuit of status or financial gain, which leads to a life that is largely devoid of enjoyment. We live in a fast-paced world that's getting faster every day. And as we've covered in a previous chapter, the pressure to keep up can seem overwhelming. But wherever your ventures take you, be careful not to engage in a lifestyle that isn't worth the price you're paying for it. For many, this can become a slow boil, and if one isn't vigilantly maintaining a healthy work-life balance, years - even decades - can slip by before the cost of that imbalance is understood and regretted. Telltale signs that you're too deep into your own personal rat race include not having time to be focused and fully present with others; not reserving time to offer help to others in ways that you feel are important; and losing the capacity to be consistently patient, courteous, or even ethical. Life isn't supposed to dictate who you are; that's up to you. If you begin to feel that you're being unconsciously influenced by life, it's time to stop and ask yourself some important questions about your priorities, your pursuits, and how much is enough.

Now that we've covered overdoing the pursuit of "enough," let's talk about the opposite dynamic. Absent-mindedness is the silent thief of "enough." Whether it concerns enough money, food, worktime, playtime, or sleep, this formidable force doesn't discriminate. When we aren't paying attention, so much can slip through the cracks. Examples include spending money indiscriminately, wasting food by over-purchasing or over-ordering, allowing oneself to become a workaholic, and getting lost in our screens as endless videos and social media posts eat up sizable swaths of our time and our sleep. I personally know someone who can't remember the last book they read after downloading a popular social media app, and that was several years ago. Please don't read this the wrong way. Diversions and entertainments can be healthy, inspiring pursuits. But if we hand our diversions a blank check without setting boundaries and limits, those diversions will grab control, and we'll be living less of a life because of them.

The Solution:

The most effective way to create enough of anything in your life is to recalibrate how you're living. Here are three ways that can help:

1) Practice gratitude every day. However little time or resources you think you have, there are many others who have far less. A daily recognition of the good things you have automatically shifts your frame of mind into abundance. This will prevent a perception of scarcity that can negatively color your vision of the world and block hidden opportunities from your sight. In the card game of life, we're all dealt different hands of abundance. And the less you blame the dealer (life), the better you'll play the hand you've been dealt. Remember, as with any card game, an initially abundant hand can lose, just as an initially sparse hand can win.

2) Share. This act doubles down on the abundance mindset and helps create more abundance. When you share even a little of whatever you have, it trains your subconscious to think more optimistically about your circumstances, and optimism tends to attract greater opportunity. Also, sharing is a compassionate and gracious thing to do, and grace is attracted to the gracious.

3) Once again, prioritize. Start with your health. You are the locomotive of your life. And if the locomotive breaks down, the whole train stops. It may seem selfish to give your highest priority to things like eating well, exercising, and sleeping enough, but self-neglect eventually translates into life neglect. And if you run out of health - whether physical or mental - it won't do you or your loved ones any good. Beyond the basics of staying healthy, you may try using a simple A-B-C ranking system for daily tasks. When doing so, you might be tempted to go straight for your C priorities because they're usually easier and more fun. But when you accomplish your A's first, you'll find that enjoyment of the fun stuff is enhanced because a cloud of unfinished, higher priorities isn't hanging over you.

Finally, I'll offer one more tip for having enough of anything. This is a very subjective tip, as it will mean something different to everyone. Although this advice has echoed through history in various forms, Leonardo da Vinci is often credited with purportedly saying, *"Simplicity is the ultimate sophistication."* Or, put plainly, less is more. What Leo was trying to convey is that focusing on the essential and avoiding the unnecessary tends to lend more elegance, clarity, and efficiency to any endeavor (or to any design). And efficiency consistently translates into having enough.

As discussed, though, what's essential versus what's unnecessary is for you to decide. But day-to-day, you'll never know that answer unless you continue to ask yourself the question.

LIE #26: THE WORLD IS A MESS

The Deception:

Given humanity's global challenges, including famine, pollution, pandemics, wars, inequality, racism, faltering democracies, active shooters, and cyberattacks, I've often thought to myself that if this world isn't a mess, I don't want to know what a real mess looks like. It's hard to read the news and not conclude that our world is... kind of a wreck. Yes, there has been progress over recent centuries, but what grade should be given to a world in which 10% of the population is considered food insecure? It certainly wouldn't be a grade to brag about. The definition of "mess" includes descriptors such as dirty, untidy, and confusing. Yet, those same words also describe a household kitchen during the preparation of a feast for a large family gathering. It would be objectionable to equate things like famine, war, and racism to a messy kitchen. The mess we see in the world, of course, isn't just spilled ingredients and dirty cookware; suffering and hardship are unfortunate global constants. But if we're to stay hopeful, it's necessary to reframe those hardships in the context of a bigger picture.

Across our world, individual countries and cultures are trying to devise ways of living and governing that result in a grand feast for their family of citizens. The problem is that many of these populations have a very limited definition of who their family includes. As a result, an atmosphere of *"My family's benefit can come at the expense of your family"* has become far too commonplace. There are trends, however, of cultures across the globe peacefully coming together for mutual benefit. These trends seem to indicate that the hot spot messes of conflict we see are not our long-term future, and that a "feast for all" is something we're steadily working toward. But throughout this sometimes slow process, we must still contend with occasional fires of selfishness in the world's metaphorical kitchens.

The Truth:

Two of the best-known teachings of the Buddha are: 1) Life is hard; and 2) Life is transitory. In modern culture, the spirit of these two teachings is casually captured in the well-known phrase, *"This too shall pass."* That age-old wisdom reflects the reality that a mess is always temporary. And while it's true that messes can linger, an astute study of history reveals that messes and their resulting lessons fuel societal evolution. Evolution, whether planet-wide or personal, isn't easy. Sometimes it requires choosing a darker path to learn the difference between a path that leads to darkness and a path that leads to light. The Buddha taught that difficulty is built into life, but permanence isn't. Carefully considering this will lead one to a sense of faith, though not necessarily a religious faith, but faith as perceiving that a fundamental framework of reality exists which eventually coaxes all things to trend positively.

On this subject, nature can be a great teacher. In May of 1980, Washington's Mount St. Helens erupted with an explosive force of more than 500 atomic bombs. In seconds, the mountain's summit and its entire north flank (a cubic mile of rock) were blasted into super-heated ash. Within three minutes, entire lakes were pushed out of their basins, and over 200 square miles of forest were completely flattened. Now THAT was a mess. However, scientists who began studying the volcano's blast zone were amazed by nature's ability to essentially reboot itself literally from ground zero. What had once been a barren, toxic wasteland began regenerating with unexpected speed. As this primordial ecosystem struggled for a foothold, it went through violent cycles of plant and animal species skyrocketing in numbers and then dying off completely, again and again. Finally, balance was achieved, and what has become Mount St. Helens National Park is once again a flourishing wilderness.

The Solution:

As the St. Helens example illustrates, even when your world appears to be leveled into a smoldering mess, it's always possible for something new and beautiful to reestablish itself. Our world has beaten the odds by surviving everything from giant meteors to the Great Depression, and so much in between. And if you examine your own past, you'll likely see that you've beaten the odds a time or two as well.

There's a two-pronged solution for transcending the lie that the world at large - or your personal world - is an irrecoverable mess. The first step is to think bigger by trying to see beyond where things are in this moment. Use your imagination and any optimism you can access to ask "what if" questions that offer inspiring answers. Amid uncertainty, the human mind too often defaults to pessimism and despair.

For some, this can be a subconscious desire for drama, fed by a misdirected effort to feel alive. But to go beyond the dramatic-mess mentality, one must avoid surrendering to gloom. This can be especially difficult if you're surrounded by individuals who feed your gloom. You don't necessarily need to stay away from them; you only need to access the courage to reflect a better attitude in the face of their gloom. After all, hope can be every bit as infectious as gloom.

The second step in your anti-mess campaign is to address the mess. Joining the Peace Corps and altruistically shipping off to a foreign land is selfless and certainly laudable. But for most, it's sufficient to look for a mess in your immediate vicinity. Spend a morning with a park cleanup crew, volunteer at a local homeless center, sign a petition to enact legislation that'll make a positive difference, or donate a few needed items to those displaced by a natural disaster. Any small, altruistic thing you do makes the world a little less messy. You'll find, too, that when you reach out to clean up the world's messes, your personal messes become better managed. This mysterious, reflective alignment usually materializes on its own when you become a cleaner of messes.

So, at any given time, is the world a mess? Yes and no. If you look hard enough, you'll find a flaw within everything beautiful in our world. But if you look even harder, you'll find subtle beauty in everything that's flawed. The extent of your imagination, your patience, and your faith in life itself will determine how you see the world. And how you see the world will determine how you engage and experience it... along with its messes.

LIE #27: LIFE IS SCARY

The Deception:

Forget lions, tigers, bears, and sharks; there are far scarier monsters out there that are indomitable, unstoppable and, ironically, quite beautiful. One such monster is called a neutron star. These tiny stars (typically just 10 miles in diameter) emit pulsing, brilliantly-colored light, which dazzles astronomers. Neutron stars are so dense that a teaspoon of their material weighs as much as 40,000 cruise ships. But if one of these twinkling, radioactive beauties were to form in our stellar neighborhood (within about 100 light years), it would largely destroy Earth's atmosphere, trigger an ice age, and cause planetary mass extinctions. And if you think the prospect of nearby neutron stars is scary, their big brothers, known as black holes, are by far the most terrifying monsters in the known Universe. Their extreme gravity swallows light, bends space, and stretches time. In fact, if you were to park a spacecraft on the very edge of a large black hole (without falling in), for every day you spend there, 100 years or more would pass back on Earth. Any star or planet that wanders too close to one of these phenomena is devoured and torn apart on a sub-atomic level. Scared yet? If not, then let's pile on top of these dark star doomsday devices the recognizable threats that humanity has created for itself: financial market collapses, environmental demise, nuclear Armageddon, et al.

All of this is arguably a strong case for life as a human to be a terrifying prospect. But like watching a scary movie or walking through a staged haunted house on Halloween, what we see doesn't always reflect reality, even if reality is what we're convinced we're seeing.

The Truth:

The more knowledge we have, the less scary life becomes. To illustrate this, let's talk about space rocks - big ones. NASA has a department which finds, tracks, and assesses the threat of asteroids and comets that travel through our solar system. Years ago, I read a sensational headline from an obscure news source proclaiming that a huge asteroid was hurtling toward Earth. While it was true that an asteroid was heading in our general direction, the article conceded (after a few dramatically written paragraphs) that the space rock *might* not hit us. Conveniently omitted from this article was NASA's official analysis of that asteroid, published years before the article was written, which concluded that this asteroid was on the smaller side, and there was zero chance of it impacting Earth. Anyone who read that headline, however, would've experienced unnecessary fear and stress if they hadn't, a) considered its source; b) known about NASA's asteroid tracking department; and c) understood that if a huge asteroid were going to hit us, that story would've been the only headline on every credible, major news outlet.

The bright side of getting stressed and scared after being deceived is that the experience prompts us to further educate ourselves. And combining experience with greater knowledge is what leads to wisdom. Falling for life's illusions is a rite of passage; it's why babies often cry when they hear fireworks. They don't understand that there's no reason to be afraid. And similar to the eventual appreciation of fireworks, many of our fears will become thrilling experiences as we grow in wisdom and maturity.

Life isn't scary. Ignorance is what's scary. Often, what we initially perceive as chaos is later discovered to have pattern and purpose. Buried within our fear and confusion are answers to life's greatest mysteries. Yes, we must dig for those answers, and that digging requires courage and effort. This effort, though, is always worth it. It's no fun living in fear of a world we mistakenly perceive is out to get us. But as awareness expands, fear diminishes. And one day, with our expanded awareness, we'll all discover that the cold, ruthless world we once perceived is and has always been conspiring for our growth and our evolution.

The Solution:

While it is true that life isn't inherently scary, it is full of obstacles which, if engaged carelessly, can lead to scary experiences. There are some who go to extreme lengths to avoid life's obstacles, often to the detriment of enjoying their own life. One of the most common obstacles is the trap of becoming so scared of death and adversity that one ends up living life behind an emotional - or in some cases, literal - fortress. This is the realm of paranoia. The antidote for paranoia is prudence, yet prudence can be subjective. For example, if you're afraid of contracting a virus, one option is to wear a mask in crowded places, and another is to wear a full hazmat containment suit whenever stepping foot outside your door. A good way to determine if you're being prudent or paranoid is to gauge the level of fear behind your actions. Even if your precautions are a bit excessive but you're acting courageously despite your fear, you're heading in the direction of prudence. It's only when you make no effort to push against the envelope of your fear that it becomes your overlord, and the inevitable slide into paranoia begins.

As mentioned in the previous chapter, there's tremendous value in responding through action to something you don't like. When you act with prudence in response to what scares you, that centers your mind in a more peaceful place. This peace comes from realizing that, although you can't control the world, you can choose how you respond to it without being controlled by it. This gives you greater capacity to act prudently.

So, yes, don't run with scissors, don't play golf in a thunderstorm, and perhaps wear the occasional mask and take extra vitamins during flu season. Calculating a worst-case scenario and acting prudently aren't signs of paranoia; paranoia arises when all you think about is the worst-case scenario, and nothing you do or don't do subdues that fear. Those who live in paranoia - or even intermittent fear - don't yet understand their fundamental nature. We all have the "right stuff" to thrive amid life's challenges. The primary reason we're here is to discover more of our unlimited potential every day. We are all unsinkable ships eternally sailing on an endless ocean of infinite adventure. And although we dip under the waves from time to time, buoyancy is the natural state of our soul.

LIE #28: YOU ONLY LIVE ONCE

The Deception:

This lie was saved for last because it's perhaps the most confining of them all. For many, it's also a source of significant anxiety - an anxiety that slowly increases with each passing year. Science - and in many cases, religion - teach us to believe that we are only the person we see in the mirror. Only one gender, only one race, only one body, only one face... and the list goes on. Whether you have a religion-based fear of damnation on judgment day or an agnostic fear of oblivion, it's hard to avoid a sense of missing out on a more diverse (or perhaps ideal) human experience as your life concludes. In addition, it's difficult to avoid repetitive, counterproductive thoughts like, *"If I had only done this instead of that, or chosen this over that."* This type of obsessive, hindsight chatter can be very agitating.

Although, the experience of regret can be beneficial, as it informs our future decisions.

But what if the concept that we only live once is a learned fallacy - a fallacy so ingrained in our culture that it overrides our innate, intuitive feeling that we're more than just this one character? What if life is a never-ending story which stretches into the past and into the future in ways our minds can scarcely grasp? What if this one life of which we're conscious is only a small part of our fantastic journey across countless lifetimes... lifetimes of gain and loss, growth and evolution, wisdom and experience, adventure and creation?

To adequately probe what many believe is the grand deception of living only once, we must scientifically dig into two of the most profound phenomena we experience as human beings: consciousness and time.

The Truth:

Consciousness

It's something we all share, yet no one really understands what it is or where it comes from. Science explains how the neural wiring and chemical interactions in our brains function, but science can't explain why we have the experience of a conscious mind - an impression of being aware that we are aware. The world's philosophical and scientific communities are somewhat divided on this issue and have settled into a few different camps.

"Materialism" refers to the belief that physical matter is all there is, and by some unknown process, consciousness is spontaneously created by the brain. "Dualism" is a school of thought which contends that matter and consciousness are two separate entities that are somehow temporarily joined in life and subsequently separated at death. But in this debate, there's also a third philosophy called "panpsychism," and it theorizes that consciousness is an inherent trait of matter. It suggests that everything - including microbes, rocks, plants, animals, people, planets, and stars - possess consciousness in some form. Panpsychism doesn't suggest that rocks necessarily think. Rather, it implies that even simple, inanimate matter has a subjective and unique conscious experience of some kind. It further theorizes that an expansion of consciousness occurs when matter comes together with increasing complexity, like in a human being. At first pass, panpsychism may sound a bit kooky; however, an impressive cadre of Nobel Prize-winning philosophers, mathematicians, and physicists (Bertrand Russell, Max Planck, and Erwin Schrödinger, to name a few) have endorsed this idea. Even today, an increasing number of notable, contemporary scientists are also taking panpsychism seriously.

Like these scientists, if you're inclined to consider that consciousness is fundamental to matter, then you must also consider that - since matter can neither be created nor destroyed but only changes form - your consciousness also can neither be created nor destroyed. This implies that the essence of who you are - your conscious self - is immortal and continues beyond life as you currently perceive it.

Time

Like consciousness, time is a misunderstood aspect of life. According to physicists like Albert Einstein, time is impossible to define without including space. It's observable that the way we experience time is directly affected by our velocity through space. This is why physicists refer to *"space-time"* when talking about the physical Universe. Many physicists believe that time (as part of the fabric of our Universe) is not something in motion that passes by us; rather, we're the ones in motion as we pass through the fabric of time. Things appear to age and change, of course, but according to the latest theories in cosmology, experiences in our past are not gone forever - they continue to exist simultaneously in a different part of space-time that we've already, in a sense, sailed past. Our individual experiences on this pre-existing "space-time ocean" are determined by the choices we make, along with the aspects of that ocean (or of our lives) that we choose to focus on.

If you factor these cosmological observations about time into your perspective on mortality, you may grasp that your time through this one life isn't something that expires. Instead, it represents a single voyage across an endless sea of possible experiences, circumstances, and outcomes. And like intrepid voyagers, it's not in our collective nature to embark upon just one voyage - or sail just one vessel - and then call it quits.

The Solution:

Ask questions. Not everyone shares the same perspective on what may be the biggest mystery of all. But to find *your* perspective, it can help to 1) look for answers in your own experience; and 2) look for answers in the world around you. Let's try that second one first...

Despite the enduring efforts of science and philosophy, there's still no definitive proof of reincarnation or life beyond death of the human body. However, there are many compelling cases that have been meticulously documented by several university psychiatry departments. These cases usually involve children between the ages of two and five who recall intricate details of ordinary people from past lives the children have purportedly lived. Those details often include first and last names, spouses, children, locations, occupations, hobbies, and circumstances of death. Many of these details had never been published, and they were confirmed by researchers only after interviews with relatives of the deceased individuals these children claim to have been.

Notwithstanding some elaborate ruse by their parents, it's difficult to fathom how three or four-year-olds could recall such obscure details about someone else's life so consistently. What's more, these children passed multiple tests administered by researchers who used accurate images alongside false ones in an effort to trick the children into choosing, for example, the wrong former spouse, co-worker, or childhood home. Assuming a lack of foul play, the probability that these very young kids would consistently pick the correct photos that match their past life claims over several rounds of testing is statistically astonishing. But to the amazement of university researchers, many children have done so flawlessly.

Beyond this clinical (albeit limited) psychiatric research, let's also consider the internal research of our own experiences and what they might represent. Look at your own history and notice how many different metaphorical "lives" you've lived. Many people would agree that who they were as a child, an adolescent, an adult, and a senior were all markedly different versions of themselves. And considering the personal knowledge gained, the influence of relationships, and the perspective-altering experiences that come standard with life, these shifts in persona seem all but inevitable. The roles we play can also influence who we are, and those can change from one day to the next. Consider, though, that the changes we experience during this life might be a microcosm of a much larger evolution occurring over many lifetimes of our soul.

To be effective scientific investigators on this subject, we must ask objective, probing questions like *"If reincarnation is a thing, why don't I remember it's a thing?"* and *"Are you kidding? I chose to come back as this person living this life with these hardships?"* To wrangle with the first question, notice that life is a process of learning, and learning is enhanced when we aren't distracted. Observe how much there is to learn as a human. You could live for a thousand years and only scratch the surface of the limitless knowledge and experiences available to us. One life - your life - represents a single mission to learn specific things and have specific experiences. As to why you don't remember choosing your current mission (or why you don't remember your other lives), would you really want that distraction while you're trying to concentrate on getting the most out of where you currently are? For most of us (with a few exceptions) that unconscious answer is clearly no. Moreover, one could argue that we'd sacrifice the thrill of discovery and the delight of surprise if we didn't voluntarily limit our awareness. Remember how much fun you had playing hide-and-seek as a kid?

The concept of voluntarily choosing hardship during a particular lifetime is tougher to reconcile. There are many in this world who obviously suffer and even more who suffer without anyone knowing. Whichever tragedies, conditions, or afflictions beset us, it can sound offensive to suggest that those who suffer have willingly signed up for it. Life, however, is filled with examples of how a difficult situation can lead to a wonderful outcome. Why, then, would any of us choose a difficult path for our own life? Because, on a grander scale, our souls yearn to know themselves fully and demonstrate that knowledge through the way we live our lives. To truly know something, we must first experience it. And the more wide-ranging that experience is, the fuller that knowing becomes. To know the light, we must also know the darkness; to heal suffering, we must know what it is to suffer; to be strong for others, we must know how it feels for others to be strong for us; and to find the truth, we must traverse the caves of ignorance.

It's painfully obvious that a single lifetime is woefully inadequate to appreciate the breadth and depth of what it means to be human. There are several well-meaning religions that aggressively dispute this and want to "save you" from such ideas. That "saving," however, usually comes with the threat that if you don't subscribe to their beliefs, you'll suffer for all eternity. But if you check all their belief boxes, they'll promise you a blissful eternal life. The flaw in their doctrine is this: They're trying to sell you something you already have. It doesn't matter who you are, what you've done, or how medieval your soul's current stage of growth may be; nothing and no one can take away your adventurous, wonder-filled, eternal life. And despite what you believe in or don't believe in, *you* couldn't take your immortality away from yourself, even if you tried.

Contemplating that you have eternity to live takes the disappointment out of how impossible it is to squeeze every last experience you desire into one life. It can also help tame the beast of depression, because depression is kept alive, in part, by thoughts of despair about a hopeless future. Thinking instead about bright, limitless possibilities across an eternity has the potential to shatter that despair. In fact, contemplating immortality may enhance the enjoyment of your present life. It can enable you to slow down, relax, and savor where you presently are because you know there's so much more ahead of you. And note how inspiring it is to take the leash off your imagination: With endless lives in your future, imagine the various forms you could inhabit, the different places you could live, the variety of occupations you could have, the countless forms of love you could enjoy, and the vast scope of societies you could help build. Your opportunities to explore, learn, and grow become boundless. Furthermore, it becomes laughable to compromise your values or your integrity to achieve a specific result. When any experience you can imagine is on your eternal menu, what would be the point in compromising?

And why not let your imagination *really* stretch its legs? Armed with the theoretical physics theories about space-time that we discussed, contemplate if it were somehow possible to go back and live lives in what we know as the past. Would you do anything differently with the Queen Victoria, Christopher Columbus, or Thomas Jefferson characters? Maybe there's some incident of past suffering - on a small or large scale - that you'd like to help mitigate? And let's jump totally off the rails and ponder what you'd do if you had your present life to live over again - like an actor playing the same role in a play showing on a second night. Any improvements to your performance you'd like to try? Or maybe it's not about improving. Maybe you enjoyed a particular life so much that you'd like to live it once more - like playing a favorite golf course again or watching a favorite movie a second time. But this time, perhaps for fun, you've recruited different souls to play the roles of your parents, spouse, children, or best friends - all appearing the same but featuring different "occupiers" of their familiar physical forms.

As ludicrous as this sounds, it's important to recognize that mainstream theories in quantum mechanics postulate that there are likely an infinite number of parallel universes. What does that mean? It means that scientists don't know exactly how reality and the Universe work, but mathematics is telling them that whatever we can imagine probably isn't bizarre enough. It also means that - intuitive, spiritual insights aside - considering all that science doesn't know, the only credible answer to the reincarnation question is, *"Maybe... who knows?"*

Beyond Solutions:

When the lie of only living once falls, as it eventually will for all of us, we'll recognize this as the big reveal...

the last fallen domino of delusion. It will validate all the work we've done - both in the world and within ourselves. It will foster the warm feeling of realizing that all we've experienced has been indelibly saved to the cloud (figuratively and, perhaps, literally). It will confirm that life - at any stage of conscious development - is not futile or meaningless and cannot be wiped away into obscurity. When we see through this lie, we will simultaneously see beyond the limits we were taught to believe, beyond the boundaries we perceived as unbreakable, and beyond the horizon we once thought was finite.

Concurrent with this new understanding, it's essential to remember that one's present life should not be neglected. Responsible, compassionate choices lead to pleasant outcomes, while reckless, selfish choices lead to unpleasant outcomes. Yet we mustn't be afraid to take risks knowing that - in the grand scheme of an eternity with unending opportunities to succeed - failure is just not possible.

Although at present you might be unaware of it, you never had a beginning, and you will never have an end. You are simply and awesomely an integral part of all that ever was and all that ever will be. And you are using life in this physical world to fully know yourself while joyfully examining each piece of our infinite Universe. One by one, you hold those pieces in your heart as they whisper to you the secrets of the cosmos.

So, go on.

Live your life like there are endless tomorrows.

Because, in truth...

There are.

In case you're curious...

...I grew up in Florida during the '80s and was raised in a restaurant family. Although I had early aspirations of becoming a restaurateur, I felt a strong desire to explore seemingly unanswerable questions: *What is the purpose of a human life? Where does joy really come from? What truths lie beyond our five senses?* As a young man, I went off to college and graduated with a business degree. But a drive for higher wisdom kept me constantly studying the world's greatest spiritual and philosophical texts, as well as the teachings of modern-day sages and revered historical figures.

After college, I explored a few different careers. I was a police officer, a middle school science teacher, a restaurant manager, and a private safety inspector. During this time of experimentation, I frequently traveled the globe, gaining perspective on different cultures and traditions. Though I was raised Catholic, my travels to Asia - and India, in particular - broadened my spiritual education to include an Eastern perspective.

Now, as a full-time author and spiritual counselor, I produce books, podcasts, and blogs that communicate what I perceive to be timeless wisdom... wisdom that has been taught over the ages but obscured by the shifting sands of our world's languages and cultures. I share this wisdom to promote self-awareness, compassion, and joy in our world. I also share resources with members of our human family who are solely focused on survival itself. A percentage of profits generated by my efforts is given to charitable organizations that directly aid the neediest people on our planet.

Whether we're talking about ending poverty, living in peace, or abolishing injustice, changing our world is easier than it seems. Like a massive mountain avalanche, enormous change occurs because of countless tiny shifts under the surface. We are those tiny shifts. The choice to change ourselves - to be kinder, more generous, and more courageous - is literally the force that changes the world. I can think of nothing more empowering and inspiring than that. Can you?

AuthorMannyGarcia.com